P9-DHP-637

FLOAT-TUBES,
FLY RODS
AND OTHER ESSAYS

CREDITS
PHOTO ON PAGE 16
By Ken Magee.
All Others by the Author.

LINE DRAWINGS
In Part I-II-III
By Pete Wilson and Frank Wilkens.
Entomology and Fly Pattern Line
Drawings by the Author.

COVER DESIGN
By Pete Wilson

EQUIPMENT • TECHNIQUE • FISH • ENTOMOLOGY AND FLYTYING

FLOAT-TUBES, FLY RODS
AND OTHER ESSAYS

By
MARV TAYLOR

Edited By
JAMES L. DEAN

1979

COPYRIGHT 1979 BY
MARV TAYLOR
BOISE, IDAHO

Lithographed and Bound in United States of America
By The CAXTON PRINTERS, Ltd.
Caldwell, Idaho
134750

Dedication

This book is dedicated to all those who
believe in Option II.

Contents

PART IV, ENTOMOLOGY AND FLYTYING

Prologue . . .

Legacy for Joel

Option I

The small boy walked slowly along the water's edge. Here and there he could almost see through the heavy sewage sludge, but try as he might, he couldn't see any fish.

His great-grandfather had spent several hours the previous evening recounting adventures of his youth — the fishing, hunting, camping. His grandfather had said that back in the "old days" you could take a sleeping bag, walk through the forest and stop and camp where and when you wanted.

No more. Public land had been vandalized so much in the late 1900s that the government finally closed everything. On the few lakes that still had fish, you needed a reservation, which sometimes took two or three years to obtain.

Joel looked down at the strange "fly rod" his great-grandfather had given him for his birthday and wondered if Shelby would know what it was.

He remembered his great-grandad's stories about fishing; how as a small boy he had fished the river and caught trout with this strange fly rod; how he would tie an imitation fly on the end of the line and a trout would come up and grab the fly in its mouth.

In his mind's eye, Joel tried to imagine using the fly rod in the river. It was impossible to conceive of fish swimming in the ink-black water. It was even more difficult for him to want to catch one.

As Joel neared the main bridge, the odor of the river seemed much stronger. He had forgotten to bring his breathing mask. Walking alongside the river was bad enough, but crossing the bridge could be a bad experience when the river was being flushed out.

He tried to hold his breath as he crossed the bridge, but before he reached the last span he had been forced to gasp for air. His head was spinning and he was retching as he climbed the steps to Shelby's house.

Shelby's mother took one look at Joel and immediately put him in a sleep tube. Thirty minutes of pure oxygen brought him nearly back to normal. He then showed his friend the fly rod.

"What will you do with it?" Shelby asked. Joel didn't have an answer and a call to lunch ended the conversation. After they had eaten, the two boys went down to the family room to watch TV. They became bored when the afternoon news came on with election reports.

The bond election to "pipe the river" was predicted to be very close. Joel couldn't understand anyone wanting to keep the river as it was. Everywhere else cities have buried their stinky streams. He was almost sorry for people who lived by big lakes and the oceans. They really had it bad. Joel wondered why they didn't all move to his beautiful valley. Some days you could almost see the mountains across from the mill.

He remembered his father telling his mother the mill would soon double in size. This would cause more smoke, more people, more road machines, and possibly ruin their beautiful valley. His Dad had said it was progress, and the town had to grow.

Joel turned off the TV and told his friend about the birthday present from his parents.

"You're finally going to Sun Mountain!" Shelby said. Then for the thousandth time he described his trip to the "mountain."

"It takes all day just to get to the check station. Then you get in this tram and up you go. Wow! What fun to sail up through the smog. When you get to 10,000 or 11,000 feet, you break into the bright sunlight. It's so bright, your eyes hurt even though you are wearing those strange glasses."

"Of course you could be unlucky and have clouds cover the mountain." Shelby said. He and his family had made the trip three times before they actually saw the sun.

It was late afternoon and since it was his birthday, Joel wanted to be home when his father returned from work. He borrowed a breather mask and bid Shelby good-bye.

On his return crossing of the river bridge, Joel stopped in the center span and looked down at the putrid water. Once again he tried to imagine fishing the river with his great-grandad's fly rod. Somehow the idea seemed repulsive. As he turned to continue his journey he lost his grip on the rod, and it fell into the murkey depths. He stood for a moment shaking his head, then with a sigh, he thrust his hands deep in his trouser pockets and shuffled off towards home.

Even if a fish could survive in that awful brine, he wouldn't want to catch one. If the election went right, the river soon would be underground. Anyway it was his birthday and with a trip to Sun Mountain in the offing, what else could a 12-year-old boy really hope for.

Option II

The scene: A western trout lake.

The characters: A small boy wading a shallow bay, casting a small spinner and a white-haired old gentlemen deftly dropping a fly near the rising fish.

The boy hooks a fish, plays it out, lands it . . . and releases it. A smile crosses the old man's weathered face. His thoughts drift back to an evening many years earlier: A meeting room filled with sportsmen and Fish and Game Department personnel.

10

Speaker after speaker rises and states his views on the future mangement of one of the state's key fisheries. The words are heated.

Two points of view are represented; each side is convinced it is the chosen spokesman for the people.

The old man smiles again as he remembers how his blood pressure rose as the "other side" tried to ram its ideas down his throat. He too had taken a turn in front of the group to "educate" the opposition.

So much water has gone under the bridge since that meeting that he can't remember which fishery they were arguing over. "It really doesn't matter," he muses aloud. "We got the job done or Joel and I wouldn't be here catching trout."

The old man could feel the chill of the lake penetrating his waders and he began working his way to shore. Carefully placing his prized Payne rod out of harm's way, he sat down and leaned back against the stump of an old cottonwood.

His thoughts again drifted into the past. He had fished this lake as a boy . . . again as a young man . . . and now, half a century later the lake really hadn't changed. He remembered his father showing him how to thread a worm on his snelled hook and how to curl salmon eggs on the hook so they would last at least until a fish nibbled.

"I think this is the spot," he said aloud for only himself to hear. "This is where I broke off the 'shark.'"

He looked around to make sure he was alone. Some folks think talking to oneself is a sign of old age . . . and he didn't admit to any such thing.

He reached down to gather up a handful of the lake water. It sparkled in his palm, and he was almost tempted to drink it. "No," he said to himself, "it's not quite that pure." He made a mental note to write another letter to the local newspaper, thanking former Fish and Game commissioners for instituting quality fishing regulations a quarter century earlier. He knew that had they not taken positive action in the past, he and the boy wouldn't have the fishing they now were experiencing.

He watched the boy hook another fish and could tell by the bend in the rod it was larger than the fish they had been catching. When the fish jumped Joel shouted with joy. The old man was tempted to offer his grandson help . . . but he held back. The youngster was quite able to handle the situation, and if the fish was as large as it appeared, Joel would want to be able to say he alone had caught it.

The boy landed the fish and without lifting it from the water, removed the single hook and released the fish.

"How big was it?" the old man yelled to the boy.

"Don't know for sure, Grandpa," said the boy, who had cast again without even looking around. "It would have been a keeper last year though."

New "fish-for-fun" regulations had gone into effect on most of the state's lakes and streams, and Joel had learned not to "overhandle" the trout.

The old man recalled the battles to change the thinking of some about the new regulations. The terms "quality trout fishing" and "sport fishing" once were dirty words.

But as the state's population grew and fishery habitat decreased, it became apparent to everyone that much of the remaining trout water had to be protected, or face losing the sport entirely. In some places fishermen still could keep trout, but a two-fish limit and strict enforcement of the regulations made it difficult to fish for food.

The old man's attention once again turned to the lake. Shadows cast by the nearby mountains were beginning to reach the cove. The old man could see more fish dimpling the surface. One fish in particular began to hold his attention. The

"Glluuppp" sound it made as it took the hatching caddis pupas just beneath the surface sent a shiver down his spine.

He caught Joel's attention and motioned for him to come to shore. When the boy reached him, he handed the Payne to the youngster and pointed to the fish.

He was sorely tempted to offer advice . . . but again thought better of it. The boy knew how to cast a fly; it was just a matter of being "baptized" under fire.

The boy's first cast fell short. He stripped more line, false cast four or five times and delivered the emerger pattern about two feet from the last feeding ring. Joel wasn't prepared for what happened next. The fish snatched the fly and took to the air.

Joel remembered to hold the rod high, but forgot about the ledge he was wading on and in the excitement fell face down in the lake. A moment of terror gripped the old man until he saw the boy's right hand protuding above the surface still holding the Payne high and dry. The old man chuckled and went to help the youngster.

As the pair hiked to their camper, the old man looked back at the lake one final time. Although he had first fished it during the '30s, a time most fishermen hold in reverence when discussing the great fishing of the past, he felt today just might have been the best trip of his life.

The grinning 12-year old at his side just might have been the reason.

Introduction . . .

Wwhat is the motivation for this book? It would be convenient, and aesthetically comfortable, to credit the "old man with the patched boots, the briar pipe and the Payne rod," or to cite an inner need to express myself, in journalistic form, on fly fishing as the sophisticated sport of the more noble angler.

Nothing could be further from the truth. The "seed" for this primer on float-tube fly fishing was sown by a personal desire to more completely understand fly fishing "stillwater" and nurtured these past several years by fishing every piece of water my time and energy would allow.

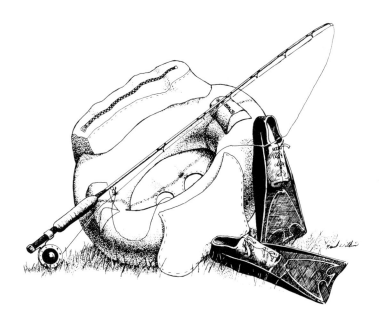

I would be less than honest if I didn't admit to a degree of selfishness in the endeavor. If there is one thing I've learned, while writing a weekly column on fishing, it is the truth in the cliche that "the teacher learns more in the teaching."

In discussing the outline of this book with my editor he asked, "Why are some grown men 'addicted' to the fishing rod?"

It's a fair question.

I've heard it said we follow the instinct of the hunter buried deep within us all. To counter-balance that theory is the one that holds we are all just "kids" who never quite grew up.

If I had to make an evaluation based on fishermen I've known over the past four decades, I'd say one hypothesis is as valid as the other.

But there is a lot more to the "fishing drive" than such simple explanations. I relate the allure of the rod to the need we all have from time to time to get away from our day to day problems and completely relax, and to excel in something other than our chosen professions.

I have yet to meet a truly proficient fishermen who wasn't proud of his skills, and who wouldn't admit, if pressured, that he probably was the best fisherman in town.

This desire to excel probably is the primary reason trout fly fisherman become fly-tyers. Unless you dress your own patterns you cannot truly control your ability to catch fish, nor can you brag with complete conviction about catching big trout on every cast — when after all it was somebody else who turned the bits and pieces of feathers and fur into the works of art that did the trick.

We could go back to the ancient Greek civilization and not find the beginning of the sport of fly fishing. Certainly the early Egyptians and Babylonians fished the fly. In some long lost cave, buried under eons of time, there may be evidence that our earliest ancestors used imitation bugs to catch their daily protein.

Contrary to the thinking of disciples of modern 20th century fly fishing experts, fly fishing as a sport goes back to the 17th century. In 1676 an Englishman named Charles Cotton added a section on fly fishing to Walton's THE COMPLEAT ANG-LER and is therefore considered by many scholars to be the father of modern fly fishing.

From Cotton's days until the late 1800s few changes occurred in equipment and fly tying techniques, or in the application of the principles of entomology relating the tied fly to the food trout actually feed on. Insect imitations almost always duplicate mayflies and were dressed to float. Even considering using a wet fly brought forth groans from the elite and nearly immediate dismissal from the hallowed halls of the Flyfishers in London.

America's Theodore Gordon for the most part continued the purist attitudes while fishing New York's Catskills. He adapted the principles of English chalk-stream entomology and technique as set down by such masters as Halford and Mar-ryat, to the streams in the Eastern United States.

English fishing writer T. E. Pritt did extensive work on wet fly fishing and generally is considered to be the man who influenced Jim Leisenring. Big Jim, the wet-fly wizard of the Broadheads in Pennsylvania, was this country's leading exponent of nymph fishing during the early part of the century.

The evolution of fly fishing technique: the liberation of the wet fly, plus vast improvements in equipment following World War II have prompted more and more fishermen to begin fly fishing.

The preponderance of irrigation and hydro-electric dams have swallowed many good trout streams, placing heavier pressure on those that remain. It became painfully obvious some years ago that fly fishermen needed to broaden their scope of activity to take up the slack.

Although history probably doesn't record who first used a pneumatic inner tube for fishing, I can remember reading about float-tubes in the 1940s. Some reports indicate float-tubes first appeared in the south — possibly Texas or Arkansas. Early tubers wore boot waders or fished "wet" and usually fished only the edges of shallow lakes.

When heel flippers evolved, the tuber became a bit more mobile. The drawback to heel flippers was the tremendous effort needed to move even short distances.

In the late 1950s a group of southwestern Idaho fly fishermen improved the design of float-tubes by adding a back rest with an extra inner tube for safety, and a stripping apron. They experimented with stocking-foot waders, scuba fins and various sinking fly lines. These fishermen developed a system of 'stillwater' fishing that allows advocates to ply the art on everything from half-acre farm ponds to giant lakes and irrigation storage reservoirs.

The float-tube offers the angler several advantages over fly fishing from a boat. The tuber has complete freedom to present his fly in whatever manner is necessary. If fish are feeding on slow moving dragonfly nymphs, right down on the bottom, he can duplicate almost the exact movement. He can use a hi-density sinking line and move his tube at almost a 'dead drift'. At times the fish will follow this type of retrieve for 50 to 100-feet before they strike. You can't effectively fish this action from a boat.

The float-tube offers the angler other more obvious advantages. Tubes are small, mobile and comfortable to fish from. They can be transported in the trunk of an average car and can be set up for fishing in just a matter of minutes.

This is not the 'complete' book on fly fishing 'stillwater'. To suggest that it is might cause raised eyebrows among fly fishermen who enjoy success with methods not outlined in this book. To describe all the techniques of fly fishing lakes and ponds would be nearly impossible. To list every successful fly pattern would make this publication cumbersome and confusing.

My goal in writing this book on float-tube fly fishing may seem like heresy to my purist contemporaries. I will simplify the art and science of fly fishing stillwater. I will remove some of the mystique from the sport and make it easy for the beginner, regardless of age or sex, to enjoy the ultimate in lake and pond angling . . . float-tube fly fishing.

I will describe stillwater entomology and how to dress patterns that "imitate" and "suggest" and also the "nondescripts," which sometimes are the most effective.

There are three basic types of lake and pond fishing. The fisherman can troll, he can anchor his boat and fish bait or flies or he can wade, casting spinners, lures or flies. The float-tube fisherman has the best of all worlds. He can troll his flies or lures if he so chooses in much the same manner as a boat fisherman, but without the speed problem that often plagues boat trollers. He can find the "high percentage" water in his lake and cast flies or lures in a more effective manner than either the boat fisherman or the wader.

Darrell Grim displays a fine specimen of Henry's Lake Rainbow-Cutthroat hybrid.

While the thrust of this book is on "fly-fishing" from a float-tube, the angler, who for whatever the reason, cannot fish the long-rod, can effectively adapt my techniques to fit his equipment. I know of several spinning-rod fly fisherman I'd hate to meet in head-to-head competition with the "family farm" at stake.

I have divided this study of float-tube fly fishing into four parts: equipment; technique; fish species and entomology and fly patterns. Although I have developed personal techniques and fly patterns, much of what I learned during my apprentice tubing days came from other fishermen. I was fortunate to have been associated, both on and off the water, with most of the pioneers of the "Idaho float-tube system." I have watched with delight as the technique proved itself on lakes all over the west.

I learned some degree of "persistence" from one of the system's co-developers, Darrell Grim. Darrell, a Nampa, Idaho television repair shop owner, best exemplifies the fishing proverb that, "He who keeps his fly in the water the longest, reaps the 'longest' reward." Darrell's reward is often the "longest trout."

I learned flytying from Boise fly shop operator, Ken Magee with whom I have fished the float-tube thousands of hours.

I learned tubing safety from Boisean Norm Bates who got me started in float-tubing.

From Twin Falls' Ruel Stayner, sporting goods dealer, rod-builder, fly-tyer, and talented angler — I learned theory and application. Ruel taught me to drop a tiny

Float-tubers are able to enjoy winter fishing by wearing two layers of insulated under-clothing, plus goose-down booties in between layers of wool socks. Although the water temperature was 39 degrees Ken Magee was able to open the Idaho stillwater trout season in January with this fine 3-pound specimen of rainbow trout.

One of the best arguments for becoming a float-tube fly fishermen are those days when fishing is so good fish in the 6-pound range can be released to fight another day. The author releases a fine Montana rainbow.

white popper along the tule beds for bluegill and to disregard tradition in dressing my stillwater nymph patterns.

I learned humility from Californian Hal Janssen. The fly rodder who hasn't fished with Hal at Henry's Lake, watching him "rip" out fish after fish while everybody else is drawing a blank, has a new form of "water torture" in store.

The enjoyment an angler can derive from float-tube fishing is difficult to put a price tag on.

I recall a day several years ago when I was tubing Pyramid Lake in Nevada. A 26-foot trolling boat, containing eight or ten anglers, floated up next to where I was fishing and we chatted. After a few "snide" remarks about my "cheap" equipment, I asked the owner if his boat might be worth as much as $20,000. He admitted that was a "ball-park figure." I then told him that if I could never again purchase another float-tube, I would be unwilling to trade him straight across for his boat.

He left muttering something about, "that screwball nut from Idaho."

I'm not sure but what that wasn't the day this book was "spawned."

PART I
EQUIPMENT

Chapter 1

The Float-Tube

Float-tubes have developed from humble beginnings on a southern bass pond to a sophisticated fishing system for thousands of western trout fishermen.

The "system" begins with a 20-inch truck inner tube, which is inflated inside a cover of canvas or vinyl-coated nylon. The shell has a saddleseat in which the angler sits wearing chest high, stockingfoot waders.

Most commercially built float-tubes have equipment pockets on either side and a backrest with an extra inner tube for safety. The complete tube also has a flap that covers the tuber's lap and serves as a stripping apron.

Besides the shell, inner tube, and waders, the float-tuber must have a means of locomotion. Two choices are available. The simplest, most efficient, and most widely used method is scuba fins. By raising and lowering his legs the tuber can

It requires very little effort to move the tuber. The fisherman sits in a comfortable, upright position, moving to the rear. It is the easiest method to fish the nymph or streamer.

move backwards with comparative ease. Although this might seem awkward at first, the stillwater nymph fisherman soon realizes that moving "backwards" is the "right" way.

Paddlepushers — hinged fins that strap onto the heels — are the other choice. By swinging his legs back and forth with the paddlepushers attached the float-tuber can move forward or sideways. I only recommend paddlepushers for small ponds where the fisherman, in fishing dry flies, hair bugs or poppers, needs to move forward. If the tuber needs to travel great distances he soon will recognize the value of scuba fins, particularly the over-sized variety.

For comfort, the tuber needs insulated underwear and down-filled booties for the cold water he fishes in spring and fall and a rain slicker to protect against rain or wind-driven waves.

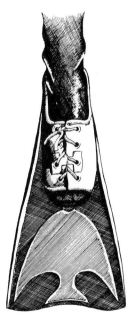

Many tubers use laced scuba fins that allow the use of heavy socks and down-filled booties for extreme cold weather fishing.

Float-Tube Safety

Man has hunted and fished throughout history. If he didn't hunt or fish for his living, he did so in the name of sport. The New England whaler in his small boat, with lance fastened to a many ton whale, is not unlike the New Zealand bill fisherman although each probably would question the other's sanity.

Some people also view float-tubing with raised eyebrows. I was launching my tube on a valley pond one day when an elderly gentleman asked me if it wasn't a "real dangerous way to fish?"

"What do you do when (not if) you spring a leak?" He asked.

I've written many times in my newspaper column that the float-tube may be the safest method of lake and reservoir fishing yet devised. I long ago ceased to worry about tube puncture and would prefer to ride out a serious storm in a tube than in most 14- and 15-foot boats.

After my conversation with the elderly gentleman, I researched my logs to check the dangerous moments I've had during 40 odd years of fishing and hunting. My research revealed that although I've been actively involved with water, weapons and other potentially dangerous situations for most of my life, my "narrow escapes" usually were more amusing that perilous. Most were unusual situations or simply

Float-tubers enjoy fishing where boats with motors aren't allowed.

where I lost control of things through carelessness. As with 99.9 percent of private aircraft accidents, "pilot error" was the chief culprit.

To people who worry that the float-tube is unsafe, I offer the following testimony on the relative safety of float-tubes and boats.

On a trip to a favorite trout reservoir in Nevada, I was tubing along the shore when a 12-foot aluminum boat trolled by. I overheard the following conversation:

"My God, I wouldn't go out in the water over my head in just an inner-tube."

"Should be outlawed."

"What idiot would use such a thing? (Float-tube)"

As the 12-foot boat moved past, I noticed four things: six persons were in the small craft; only the two children were wearing life-preservers; the small boat was under-powered with an ancient 5-hp outboard; and, thunderclouds were gathering in the south.

The Rules

The key to safety around water is good common sense. A few simple rules must be followed when fishing the float-tube.

Number one on my list of cautions is an "absolute." DO NOT fish any type of moving water in a tube. The possibility of being pushed under a log or some other

23

obstruction or being over-turned by a shallow bar offsets any potential fishing success. The float-tube was designed for stillwater . . . that's where it should be used.

Rule number two is not always easy to follow. Tubers should always try to fish with a buddy. About the only time a float-tuber is in any real danger is when he is entering or leaving the water. It is a good idea to have a person nearby in case you lose your footing.

Rule number three: When using scuba fins always back in and out of the water watching for rocks, logs, muddy spots, etc. If you feel yourself stumbling, quickly sit down in your tube.

Rule number four is to watch for storms with heavy winds and/or lightening. Although a tuber can "ride out" heavier winds than most boaters, I recommend watching storms from shore.

Rule number five is more for comfort than safety. Dress more warmly than you think is necessary. A tuber can be fairly comfortable in water temperatures as low as 38 or 40 degrees if he is properly dressed. In extremely cold water, I wear two pairs of insulated underwear, two pairs of wool socks and goose-down booties.

On the subject of comfort, I also strongly recommend the tuber avoid the over-use of beverages — particularly alcoholic beverages. Besides the more obvious problem of unavailable "rest stops," alcohol lowers the body temperature and can cause problems in cold weather.

I also urge the use of a good sunscreen lotion on bright, sunny days.

Rule number six: Although the better 20-inch float-tubes, particularly the custom-made models, have an extra pocket on the back that holds an extra inner tube, I recommend wearing an inflatable safety belt or life jacket.

Rule number seven is a very simple rule, but it can save a fishing trip. Since "volume" is the criteria for inflating float-tubes and not "pressure," the tube should be soft to the touch when fully inflated.

When transporting tubes to higher elevations, remember the accompaning low pressure can cause tubes to expand and over-inflate. Release air from the float-tube before you go to a high country lake.

My eighth rule isn't aimed at safety, unless you have short-fused anglers fishing on shore. Always keep well out of a claim on any water they can reach with their cast. Let them have that much . . . and more.

Chapter 2

Rods and Reels

The recent trend has been toward longer and softer rods, but the float-tuber need not invest heavily in new rods to be well equipped. In most fishing, he doesn't need to make super long casts and can get by with shorter rods than stream fishermen. Since most lake and pond fishing is with nymphs, wet flies and streamers, he can buy one rod for most of his stillwater trout fishing.

My first fly rod, discounting the steel telescopic model I learned to fish with during the Great Depression, was an inexpensive, imported split bamboo that lasted less than a year.

My second fly rod was one of the first fiberglass models sold in my home town of Nampa, Idaho. I fished with it for over 20 years, and it still is in excellent condition.

I retired that rod, and since then have purchased — or built — about a dozen fly rods. I doubt any of my rods ever will be "worn out." It isn't that I don't fish enough — one thing I've never been accused of is hobby neglect — but about the time I get acquainted with a new rod, an improved model is introduced that I "have" to try.

I guess I'm among the "fly rod — nut brigade" who own closets full of rods but drool every time a Payne shows up in a fly fishing catalog. Lately I've had my eye on this neat 8-foot split bamboo that would fit my number six lines . . .

Beginning fly fishermen are confronted with three basic types of fly rods: fiberglass, graphite and bamboo. The latter two types can be quite expensive, so I would advise the beginner to buy fiberglass. He should purchase the very best rod he can afford. Many excellent production rods are available in most full-line sporting goods stores.

The beginner should buy a medium-action rod in either 8- or 8½-foot for a number six or seven line. For youngsters, or people with less physical strength, I recommend a 7½-foot rod for either a five or six line.

If the tuber gets more involved with the sport, he will need other rods. Try to imagine tubing Flaming Gorge for 30-pound browns with the same fly rod used for bluegills and crappie. My personal arsenal of fly rods might be a guide for the dedicated float-tuber in selecting optional equipment.

Three rods form the backbone of my float-tube system. First is a 7½-foot, 2¾ ounce graphite with a medium-fast action that fits a number six line for most bluegill and crappie and much of my lake and pond trout fishing. This particular rod has a great deal of strength and will handle floating lines with dry flies as well as any graphite I've ever fished.

My second rod, also a graphite, was built for me by Ruel Stayner. It weighs 3½ ounces, is 8½-feet long and also fishes number six lines. It has a smooth, medium-soft action and is a great nymphing rod for lakes and streams. I use this rod extensively with floating lines and small flies in the surface film.

The final rod I consider necessary, at least for my fishing, is another graphite designed for bass bugging and big trout. I use it on lakes such as central Oregon's Wickiup Reservoir or East Lake where fish in excess of five or six-pounds are fairly

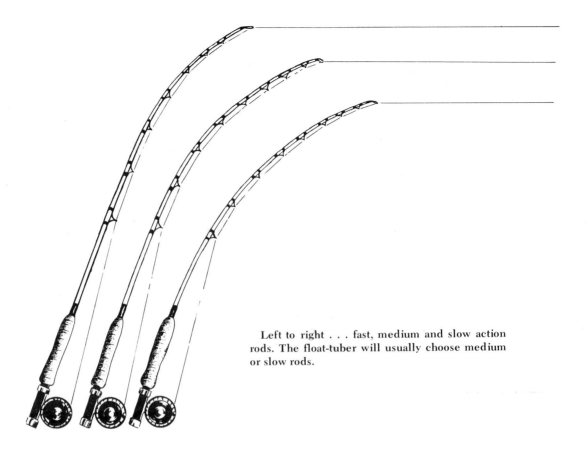

Left to right . . . fast, medium and slow action rods. The float-tuber will usually choose medium or slow rods.

common. The rod is 8½-feet long with a medium-action, weighs about 4½-ounces and will cast an 8 or 9 line a country mile . . . if I give it a chance.

There is no one "perfect" rod for all fishing conditions. Every fisherman has casting peculiarities that may or may not "fit" a particular rod. It is not my intention in this book to make "iron-clad" recommendations on tackle . . . no one can.

The arguments persist on the value of long or short rods. During the past 10 years many float-tubers went from eight-foot rods down to seven-foot. With the popularity of the newer graphite rods, we now are gradually going back to the longer rods.

I remember an article written by Lee Wulff, in which he tried to make the point that long rods are not necessary. He eliminated the rod completely. Although Lee cast his line by hand, he hooked and landed a 10-pound Atlantic salmon, playing the fish directly from the hand-held reel.

Although Lee made his point, I wouldn't recommend the technique for float-tuber. At least none with whom I'm acquainted.

Fly Reels

Fly reels also have improved during the past decade, although not as dramatically as fly rods and fly lines. The reel's chief function is balance and line storage, other than when directly involved in playing fish. It doesn't actually contribute to the cast, so it is easy to understand why manufacturers turned their efforts toward improving rods and lines.

The primary difference between inexpensive and expensive single-action fly reels — and I do not recommend automatics under any circumstances — is the degree of tolerance, smoothness of action and weight of the reel in relation to other reels of a similar size. Better reels usually are lighter, made from better quality materials and usually last longer than less expensive reels.

Novice fly fishermen purchasing a first fly reel should select a reel in the medium to medium-high price range. He should be sure the reel matches the rod and make certain the reel is the correct weight. He also should be sure there is enough line capacity to allow for enough backing to protect the angler when that fish of a life-time takes his fly. The reel also should have interchangeable spools so the angler can switch lines with medium effort.

On larger bodies of water a boat is handy to transport tuber to more productive area.

Chapter 3

Lines and Leaders

The more I get involved with fly fishing, the more I respect anglers of the past. How the wet-fly pioneers managed to catch trout with the nymphing equipment of their era mystifies me.

I guess it shouldn't. They had the advantage of fishing mostly clear, bubbling brooks and rivers and were not relegated, to any degree, to fishing man-made lakes and reservoirs. Their trout, for the most part, were natives and more partial to the natural diet of the stream than to the pellet diet of hatchery-reared fish.

Although they had these advantages, their understanding of the trout's world was minimal compared with modern fly fishing knowledge. They didn't have an Ernie Schweibert, and nothing even resembling his work on nymphs to guide them. Their tackle was quite primitive compared with modern equipment — particularly fly lines and leader materials.

Stillwater fly-fisherman must achieve expertise in three areas. The first is understanding the entomology of his favorite lake and being able to duplicate this entomology at his tying vise, or being able to purchase these flies at his local sporting goods store.

Second is casting. It doesn't take a tournament champ to catch fish in a lake with a fly rod, but the proficient caster has a decided advantage.

The third factor is completely understanding fly lines, what they will (or will not) do, and when to use them. Learning about fly lines may be the most important part of learning to fly fish stillwater.

The critical elements in fishing for trout with nymphs or wet flies, in the relative order of important, are: depth fished; retrieve; leaders; and, finally, fly pattern.

The "Taylor Law" states: "The wrong fly fished where the fish 'are' might catch fish. The right pattern fished where the fish 'are not,' hasn't got a prayer." Although this reasoning might seem elementary, it is surprising how many fishermen handicap themselves by believing they have the super fly pattern that "always" catches fish — regardless of where it is fished.

Fly lines have improved greatly since the braided horse-hair models. The final obstacle to uniformity of equipment was overcome when the American Fishing Tackle Manufacturers Association (AFTMA) established fly line standards in 1961. Rods then could be built for a specific line size and the fly fisherman could be reasonably sure every brand would fit his rod.

A number six line, for example, weighs 160 grains (give or take 8 grains) no matter what company manufactures it. The first 30 feet of the "working" portion of the fly line, exclusive of any tip or taper, as measured from the very beginning of the taper, is weighed to determine the line's AFTMA number.

But what about double tapers, weight-forwards and shooting heads? Which is best for the float-tuber?

Most nymph fishermen, particularly big-water anglers, prefer weight-forward or shooting heads over double tapers. I fish both. I like the distance the shooting-heads give me when fishing big waters with big flies. But I also like the "touch" I get from a double taper when fishing small flies in the surface film. I also like the economy of being able to "switch" ends, or being able to cut the line in half to make two shooting-heads. I believe a novice should begin with a double taper and graduate to shooting-heads after he has learned to cast.

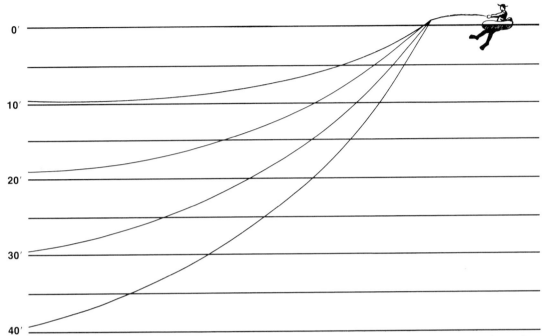

The four basic sinking lines reach various depth. Top to bottom: slow sinking lines reach to the 10 foot level; medium sinkers will go down about 20 feet; fast sinkers about 30 feet and hi-density fly lines will reach near the 40 foot level.

The six basic types of fly lines are: floater; sink-tip; slow-sink; medium-sink; fast-sink; and high-density fast-sink. Each line has its time and place, and the ardent lake fly fisherman has each line type to insure more frequent success.

When fishing Eastern Idaho's Henry's Lake, for example, the fly fisherman who doesn't have a fast sinking line often is wasting his time. The fly must be sunk nearly to the bottom so that it can begin it's upward movement just above the moss beds. With the 25-foot average depth at Henry's Lake, a standard medium-sinking line seldom will sink deep enough to get the job done.

Unfortunately not all fly fishermen completely understand this point. Each particular fly line is designed to sink to a certain level. Unless the angler uses a weighted fly or attaches some type of lead sinker to the line, a slow-sinking line seldom sinks deeper than 10 feet. A fast-sinker is limited to about 30 feet. The density of water prohibits them from going deeper.

When fish are lying in shallower water feeding on slow moving underwater life forms, the knowledgeable fly fisherman will switch to a slow-sinking line and allow his fly to dead drift along the bottom. Float-tube fishermen excel in this situation because they can lean back, wiggle their fins gently and present flies to the fish in a most seductive manner.

Another shallow water technique is using a faster sinking line with a faster retrieve to catch fish that are feeding on the "darting type" prey. I sometimes use a weighted dragonfly nymph under these conditions.

A sink-tip line is handy when trout are chasing emerging mayflies or caddis that are rising to the surface. I sometimes achieve the same action with a weighted fly on a 12- to 15-foot leader attached to a floating fly line. The best retrieve with this combination is the "Leisenring Lift."

When I'm fishing a lake I usually carry five fly lines in my equipment pocket: floater; slow-sink; medium-sink; fast-sink and hi-density. I may add a sink-tip in some situations. While it may sound like equipment "over-kill" it isn't. I strongly

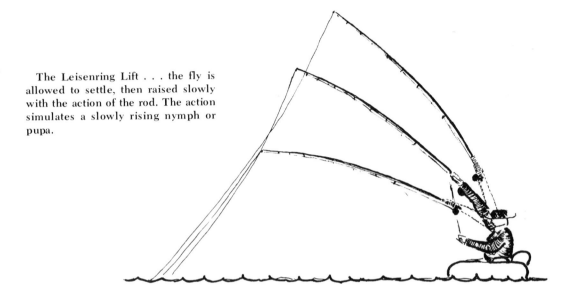

The Leisenring Lift . . . the fly is allowed to settle, then raised slowly with the action of the rod. The action simulates a slowly rising nymph or pupa.

believe in "strata fishing" and fly presentation. Don't tell me what fly the fishing are hitting — tell me the depth at which they are feeding. I'll find the fly pattern.

I recommend the beginner buy, in this order: floater; fast-sink; slow-sink; hi-density and finally a medium-sink.

Leaders

Aside from the fly or lure, the leader is one of the most important pieces of fishing tackle. You can correct for casts made with a poor rod, and even the wrong line will occasionally get the fly to the fish, but if fish are leader-shy, the best cast with the best line won't catch them if your tippet is too thick.

How long should a leader be? What material is best? How thick at the butt? How thin at the tippet? The correct answer is simple: "Long enough and thin enough to fool the fish, and strong enough to land it."

To fool a wary trout you might need a 20-foot leader one day while the next time out 36 inches would be more than enough. Some days you can use 10-pound test tippets while on other days you have to go as light as one-pound to get strikes.

Clarity of water and associated conditions usually dictate leader length and tippet strength — but not always. A few years ago I fished Montana's Clark Canyon Reservoir, and the "dirty water-heavy leader" theory went right out the window. The lake was murky with a fairly heavy algae bloom, and I thought I could get by with a medium-heavy tippet. Because the lake harbors extra-large rainbow and brown trout, I began with an 8-pound test tippet. Nothing happened.

I tried a 6-pound tippet and the 4-pound. I hooked a few fish at the 6-pound level but did much better at 4. I did not, however, land all the big ones I hooked using the lighter tippet. It was a case of reducing my leader or not getting strikes and given a choice, I'd rather hook 'em and lose 'em, than not having strikes at all.

How thick should a leader be at the butt? For most fly fishing, tapered leaders are best. Since most tapered lines come to a forward point of about .30, the diameter of the leader butt should approximate that size no matter how long or short the leader. Avoid knots wherever possible by using knotless tapers. If knots were good in leaders, they also would be good in lines . . . and they aren't.

One day we'll have united lines and leaders; that is, lines of leader material that taper smoothly from the heavy belly section to an invisible terminal diameter where the fly is tied on. Such lines, which are made of leader material, have been built experimentally but so far as I know are not for sale.

Stiffness is a factor in casting, and since leader materials are stiffer than lines, a slightly smaller diameter in the leader material gives the smoothest flow in casting. This means that a diameter of .026 to .028 inches is the best butt diameter for any leader.

The weight and air resistance of the fly to be cast affect the diameter of the leader point to which they are attached. A heavy fly, snapping hard against a fine tippet in a gusty wind, soon will break the monofilament at the knot. A small fly on a stiff and heavy tippet will not "swim or drift freely" and will not seem natural.

My preference in tubing leaders leans toward the 9-foot knotless variety tapered to .009- or .010-inch. I can then add sections of lighter tippet material giving me the 11- to 12-foot leader I prefer.

I follow one rule in most of my tackle preparations: make it easy for the fish to cooperate.

Chapter 4

Water Thermometer

Many anglers venture forth to battle the wily trout (or bass, crappie, bluegill, etc.) without one of the most useful pieces of equipment — a water thermometer.

Not one angler out of 20 totally understands the influence of water temperature on the feeding habits of fish. What water temperature sparks bluegill to begin feeding in the spring? And at what temperature do the bulls generally begin building nests? The avid bream fisherman knows the answers.

Trout anglers should know that the ideal temperature for rainbow trout is from 55 to 70 degrees. If the water is colder than 50 degrees or warmer than 75 degrees, fishing can be tough. Brook trout prefer somewhat colder water, as do cutthroats.

Aside from understanding the prime temperatures for various species, an angler should record the water temperature when important hatches occur. A callibaetis mayfly hatch on one of my favorite trout lakes, Horsethief Reservoir, nearly always triggers super fishing, and I know the hatch usually begins as the water temperature approaches 55 degrees. Early in the season the little speckled-wing dun hatches in the late afternoon. As the season progresses the hatch comes earlier in the day. The angler who knows when the water temperature reaches 55 degrees greatly improves his chances on this lake.

The massive spring midge hatches on lakes such as Clark Canyon Reservoir in Montana depends on water temperature. If an angler is close enough to such lakes

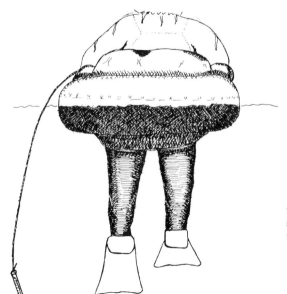

It is important to measure temperature at a constant depth. Four feet seems to give an accurate reading of water conditions.

to catalog water temperatures, over a period of several years he can predict the best fishing with a great deal of certainty.

Steelhead anglers, who fish with fly rods, know that when water temperatures drop to 40-43 degrees they do poorly with flies. Fish become less active as fall water cools and lie in holding water waiting for the spring thaws.

A two-degree rise in water temperatures in March can "awaken" steelhead, and if your fly is in the correct spot you should find action. In colder water, steelhead are often found in slower moving pools. As the water gets warmer they prefer to move to more traditional holding lies. A thermometer can "make" or "break" your steelhead fishing.

Summer trout fishing in streams is similar. When waters warm to 70 degrees trout will move from pools to riffles for oxygen. Working pools at this time of the year usually is futile.

Fishing for bass, bluegill or crappie in water colder than 50 degrees usually doesn't put much on the dinner platter. According to my records, we begin catching bluegill, with regularity, at 50 degrees. Good action comes at 55 degrees and super activity at 60 degrees.

Bluegill begin to move to their spawning beds at 70-75 degrees and are extremely vulnerable at that time.

In taking water temperature it is important to be consistant in the depth you drop your thermometer. Mine is tied to one of my tube equipment pockets with a four-foot length of cord. When I drop it over the side it always is at the same depth.

I faithfully record morning, afternoon and evening water temperatures and consult my logs on every fishing trip.

Chapter 5

The Fishing Log

For the past twenty years, I've faithfully kept a fishing and hunting log. I go back to my records to determine when channel catfish should begin feeding heavily in the spring.

I can plan a fishing trip to my favorite lowland trout reservoir when the damsels are hatching. Based on a five-year average, I can predict when the bluegill will become active and when the bass begin to spawn.

Besides aiding in catching fish, my logs are important in reliving trips of years past; where I went and what my success (failure) rate was. My logs have become more and more sophisticated over the years, and I now enter everything that can possibly be of value in the future.

On a fishing trip, for example, I record: air and water temperature; whether the barometer is rising or falling; stage of the moon; fly patterns that caught fish; identifications of insects or nymphs found on the lake or streams; stomach contents of fish that I kill, and so on.

It is interesting to study these accounts of hunting and fishing trips, and the information is invaluable. But another benefit of a well kept log, is being able to recall events incidental to the actual hunting and fishing . . . the photo of the bull moose feeding in the lily pads . . . the unusually brilliant sunset at Cascade Reservoir . . . or, the fact that our family feline Chiang, a siamese, cornered a gopher that was too big for him and ended up a "sore loser."

But in going over some of my older log-books, it occurred to me that I had often failed to enter these "non-fishing" or "non-hunting" items. It was a large error on my part.

One week-long fishing trip to eastern Idaho is a good example. The fishing was only fair . . . I didn't report any five or ten-pound trout taken from Henry's Lake or, for that matter, large quantities of rainbows from Island Park Reservoir . . . but, I will never forget the eight days Vina and I spent in the area.

First there was the moose that wasn't there. When we arrived at Staley Springs on Saturday we checked in and found our camping spot. Our neighbors informed us that there had been a moose feeding in the field next to camp for several days. Vina spent two days watching for the big animal so I could photograph it, but unfortunately a band of sheep moved in and the moose departed before I got a good shot.

One day we drove over to fish Montana's Hidden Lake. During the drive, we observed a pair of rare trumpeter swans with a brood of three cygnets nesting at the upper end of Elk Lake. I shot a half roll of film and got several good slides of the great white birds.

Seeing the swans overshadowed the fishing although we did get into a good mayfly hatch with active trout.

That same day a summer storm kept us from fishing the famous McDonald Pond, in Montana's Centennial Valley. We knew there were large fish in McDonalds and had been looking forward to casting a fly for them. Unfortunately, summer rain had turned the small draws into streams and the streams into torrents threatening at times to wash out the road over Red Rock summit.

I'll always remember the freshness of that day. I could have made a fortune if I could have bottled it and sold it to one of the water softener companies.

After several days at Henry's Lake we moved our camp to Island Park Reservoir and spent the balance of our week fishing with a group of friends from the Twin Falls area. Friendly competition marked the fishing most days, including the evening when a rank beginner who didn't know how to cast a fly, retrieve a fly, or play a fish, beat us all soundly. In fact he caught more fish than the rest of us put together.

I'll certainly remember the fishing part of the trip. What I'll recall best, however, will be the evenings around the campfire . . . the beer can hat-building binge that occupied some of the gals for the whole trip . . . the sight of the mild-mannered member of our party, who finally tired of the campground motorcycle brigade and put a stop to it once and for all with a clenched-fist approach that his adversaries could not misinterpret.

I'll not soon forget the continually serenading sandhill cranes that were nesting in the area.

Despite its trivial nature, one final bit of miscellaneous information went down in my log. I had been over the Red Rock Pass several times but on this trip Boisean Ken Magee pointed out that when crossing from Idaho to Montana at this point, the streams flowing to the west end up in the Atlantic Ocean, and the streams flowing to the east in the Pacific. Ken says it might be the only spot in the United States where this oddity exists.

While my logs are a great aid in planning successful fishing trips, I'm not sure but what they aren't more valuable for reminiscing about past adventures on a long winter evening.

Chapter 6

Devious Fishermen: An Essay

Fishermen are devious people.

How often can you walk up to an angler, ask how the fishing is and get a really straight answer?

More than likely he'll pass off your query with, "nothing to brag about," "lots of small fish, nothing big," or "not a strike in hours," . . . despite the fact that he has a pair of three-pounders under the bank.

Even relatives won't help you. I remember how long it took me to find out about Corral Reservoir, although my brother-in-law had been catching big fish there for years.

I usually dislike asking how the fishing is, because if the fish are biting I'll probably find out anyway, and if fishing is bad, I don't want to hear about it.

But the really devious fishermen are those who "manufacture stories" designed to discourage other fishermen from fishing their favorite waters. Stories about rattlesnake infestations, for instance, tend to keep the competition down.

I recall as a small boy overhearing my father and his buddies discussing a trip to the South Fork of the Boise River. They scripted their trip well, right down to the 16 rattlesnakes they saw in a two mile stretch of the river. Dad flowered his story with incidents like reaching into a sagebrush for a salmon fly and accidently catching a rattler by the tail.

I wouldn't suggest that my father was any more of a story-teller than the next fisherman, but he certainly knew how to discourage others from fishing his most productive water.

Another of our favorite trout fisheries was the South Fork of the Payette River. It always produced good fishing for the angler who was willing to climb down into the deep canyon below Lowman. Most of our friends knew where we fished but wouldn't venture into the canyon. Why? Because of a dangerous "quicksand bed" that reportedly had gobbled up at least two fishermen over the years.

I still can see the twinkle in my father's eye when he described how he almost got caught in the quicksand. We even went so far as to post a crude sign at Rattlesnake Creek warning anglers of the danger.

I suppose when you get right down to it, you can find some type of hazard to discourage fishermen from any lake or stream.

Some of my friends came up with a new wrinkle that intrigues me. A small, easily accessible lake, a hundred miles north of Boise — one that regularly produces rainbow trout up to five pounds — has, according to angling friends, recently been invaded by a family of otters. Now otters, while being fun little critters in a snow bank, can be downright wicked in the water.

Otters and float-tubes in a two acre lake? Not my float-tube.

But . . . are they really there?

Fishermen can be devious about fishing techniques as well. I know a float-tuber or two who wouldn't show you a successful fly pattern even if your life depended on it. I know several good fly fishermen who "hide" their "retrieve" as if it were the crown jewels of England.

One of Southern Idaho's best float-tubers told me the story of how he was catching fish one day on Mormon Reservoir when nobody else could get a strike. He had discovered early in the day that the fish were taking a super-quick retrieve. He would retrieve slowly — watching until his buddies were looking the other way — then, rip-rip-rip . . . fish on. It took all day for the others to catch on.

What is the morality of fishermen "story-telling" about fishing conditions to keep other anglers away from certain lakes or streams? It depends, I guess, on the spirit in which it is done and, to some extent, just how much fabrication is necessary.

To be perfectly honest, if the quality of the fishing is good enough, I can't imagine a few rattlers chasing anybody away.

But for me to put my float-tube in a two-acre lake with a family of otters . . . that's another story.

PART II
TECHNIQUE

Chapter 7

Strategy and Technique

When I first began fishing for trout, which was at a very early age, I discovered one important fact about catching fish. Trophy fish invariably are caught in the same stretches of water.

That may seem like a broad statement but the implication to an eight year old was clear because most large trout I caught from my favorite drain ditch were taken from just three or four holes. As a veteran float-tube nymph fisherman I've learned that my youthful experiences are as true in stillwater as in the drain ditch.

I've come to think of a trout's domicile as having "sleeping quarters," "leisure quarters," and a "dining room." We seldom ever catch him while he's in his "bedroom." We sometimes succeed while he's in his "living room," but if we really want the percentages on our side, we'd better find his "dining room."

Some areas in our trout lakes can be considered 95% water — areas that produce fish much more frequently than 5% water. The angler who spends 95% of his time on 95% water has mastered the most important rule in fishing: Fish where the fish are.

In streams, trout tend to congregate in feeding lanes where insects hatch. The lanes are for the most part static. Water temperature causes some fluctuations as does water volume, but once we learn where the big fish are, we usually can fish the same hot spots year after year.

Lakes and reservoirs are different. The hatches occur at different times throughout the season and at different locations. As the water level drops, in the case of storage reservoirs, anglers must search for the new feeding areas.

In the lakes and reservoirs, trout are far more migratory in their feeding habits. They have a tendency to feed more in their "living-quarters" than stream fish, but their "dining room" is wherever the hatches are, or the weed beds where shrimp and scuds can be found, or the snail beds. If there is an area in the lake where forage fish can be found in good numbers, you can usually find large trout, in good numbers.

Several years ago, I began keeping a log of where I caught the most and largest trout in my favorite lakes. I find I take greater numbers of fish when I locate them in either their "dining room" or in migratory lanes leading from their living quarters to these "dining rooms."

Generalizing on lake and reservoir trout fishing could be dangerous. Every rule has its exceptions, and in trout fishing there are exceptions to the exceptions.

One of the most frustrating exceptions is Henry's Lake in eastern Idaho. You can be sitting in the "Glory Hole" — the fishing hotspot at Staley Springs — with the right pattern, right line, right retrieve and still not get a bump all day long. The guy sitting right next to you using the same fly, same line, same retrieve . . . might be taking fish with every cast.

Henry's Lake "is" the exception that "makes" the rule. The following description of how I "attack" a lake should help the reader with all but the most exceptional situations in stillwater fly fishing.

I arrive at my favorite lake full of enthusiasm and find the water dead calm, without evidence of a hatch or rising fish. I talk with several bait fishermen at one of the hotspots on the shore and they tell me fishing was great at daybreak, but the action lasted only an hour or so. Three or four boats troll by and from the relaxed attitudes of their occupants I know they aren't catching fish either.

I decide the prospects aren't worth getting rigged up for so I get back into my car and drive home. Right? Wrong! I'm a float-tube fly fishing optimist specializing in nymphs and wet flies. What I've witnessed doesn't discourage me in the least. As a matter of fact it has given me several clues.

I know that I must follow the first rule in fishing if I'm to be successful. I must

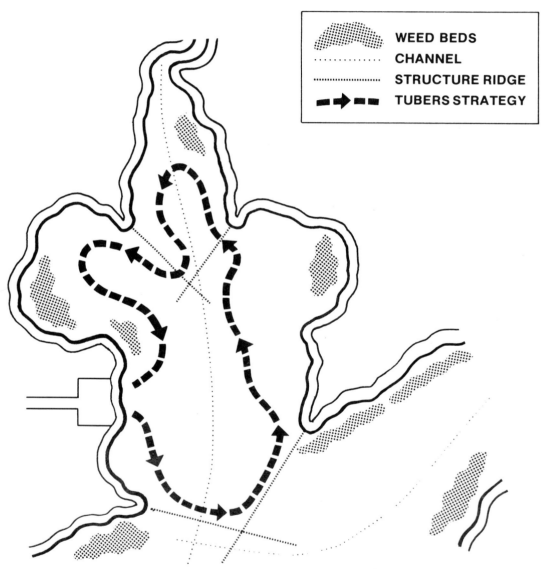

WEED BEDS
CHANNEL
STRUCTURE RIDGE
TUBERS STRATEGY

Beginning at the launch site the float-tuber searches down the first structure ridge and then up the second. If he hasn't found fish by this time he will swing out to deeper water, following the channel to the next structure ridge. He will search out the shallow water near weed beds as well as the fourth structure ridge. He will continue to follow this pattern until he discovers the area, and the depth fish are feeding.

put my fly where the fish are . . . it's as simple as that. The greatest presentation with the rod . . . or the most precisely tied fly pattern . . . or the super bait of all time . . . won't catch fish, if fish aren't there to be caught.

I mate my rod to a reel loaded with a fast-sinking line. I place four other spools — containing a floater, a slow-sinker, a medium-fast-sinker and a hi-density — in the pocket of my float-tube. The pocket also contains extra leader material, hook hone, leader clippers, water thermometer and several boxes of flies.

Structure Ridge

Fish will seek out various types of cover. Points of land that offer "structure ridges" are good examples. The float-tuber should position his "drift" 20 to 30 feet on the down-wind side of the ridge and cast across it. Fish will be lying facing the movement of the water, watching for drifting food.

As I tube along the "structure ridge" closest to the campsite I probe each side carefully. (note drawing) My first offering to the trout will be a dark olive green pattern in size eight. It might be a Tex's Favorite, a dragonfly nymph, a thorax nymph or a woolly worm. When I get out over deeper water I let my line sink deeper and use a very slow retrieve — almost a dead drift. If after five or six casts something hasn't happened, I gradually speed up my retrieve. I try several variations until I eventually reach the "super quick" line recovery.

This brings me to the second most important rule in float-tube fly fishing, or any type of fishing for that matter: Do not be afraid to experiment. More often than not it is the depth you are fishing, and the speed of your retrieve that catches fish.

If I haven't caught fish after 15 or 20 casts I change patterns. In order of presentation I will go through: dark olive, dark and light brown (probably a leech pattern), light olive (possibly a damsel imitation), tan, gray and black. The flies are mostly simple nymph and wet fly patterns ranging in size from 6 through 14 — including: damselfly nymphs; dragonfly nymphs; mayfly nymphs; caddis larva and pupas; midge larva and pupas, and leeches.

If I still haven't caught fish I move into the intermediate depth water using shrimp, snails and streamer patterns.

Don't just troll aimlessly around the lake "hoping" to catch fish. Look for areas near the inlets, particularly if there are weed beds, where fishing can be good. Also look for weed beds and shallow water where nymphs and forage fish will be more

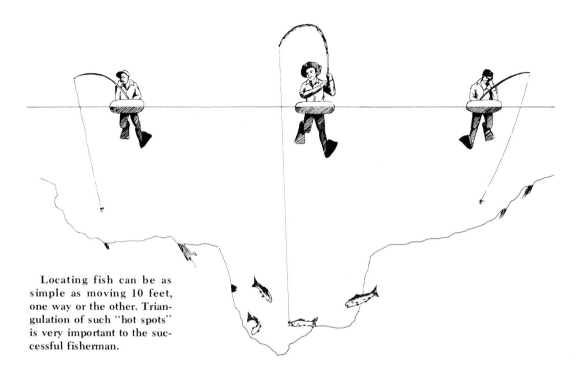

Locating fish can be as simple as moving 10 feet, one way or the other. Triangulation of such "hot spots" is very important to the successful fisherman.

numerous. Fish use the shallows that are away from the actual shoreline whenever possible.

When you do locate a hotspot, "triangulate" its location with shore objects and never forget it.

If, after fishing several hours I still have not caught fish, I try something different. I go with attractor patterns, maybe a "ducktail," marabou muddler or coon-bug. I go "big and ugly, little and dainty." I fish fast, and I fish slow. I continue to watch other fishermen for signs of activity.

Late evening should provide a hatch if one is going to occur. I watch the shore line for any tell-tale swirl of feeding fish. I change again to the slow-sinker (or floater) and work the weed beds near shore.

As darkness falls, I realize I have tried everything. I have lengthened my leader to 15 feet, and I have reduced the size of my tippet to three-pounds. I've touched all the bases and still haven't caught fish. I tube to shore and look back on my favorite lake — at least it used to be — and vow tomorrow will be different.

It usually is.

Chapter 8

Imagination — The Key

A fishing companion once made an interesting observation on a Memorial Day outing to Sheep Creek Reservoir on Nevada's Duck Valley Indian Reservation. The fishing had been spotty. Two one-hour periods had provided only fair fishing, and my companion observed that, "fishing when it gets tough can be more rewarding than when it is too easy."

On the surface his philosophy was easy enough to understand, but carried out to it's conclusion, you would have to say, "not catching fish is more fun than catching fish." At that point I part company with my friend's philosophy. As noble as his attitude might be, it does wear a bit thin carried to extremes.

The fishing at Sheep Creek wasn't really that slow, but it came in spurts, and you had to be at the right spot at the right time. Early morning fishing was slow until the surface water warmed and produced a good mayfly hatch.

I had good action with a "stick fly" in three or four feet of water using a variation of the "Leisenring Lift" retrieve. I attached my fly to a 12-foot leader on a floating line. I would cast, count to 10 to allow my weighted fly to sink near the bottom and then slowly lift my rod to the vertical position. If I detected even the slightest hesitation in my line I would strike. If not, I lowered my rod to the water, retrieved the slack line and repeated the "lift."

My "stick fly" probably imitated the emerging callibaetis mayfly nymph, which is a speckled wing variety common to most western lakes. My technique produced results during the evening, except I had to switch to a hare's ear nymph.

"Tomorrow we'll murder them," I advised our group at the evening campfire.

The next morning, however, repeated the previous day's dilemma . . . no fish until noon, then the same callibaetis hatch.

I was using the same rod, reel, line, leader, tippet and fly pattern. All conditions were "go" except nobody told the fish. They stayed in deeper water, and it took a deep-sinking line and an entirely different approach to catch fish.

I would like to be able to predict, with reasonable certainty, what turns fish on. I can't — nor can anyone. There are too many factors to consider: air temperature; water temperature; barometric pressure; cloud conditions; wind conditions; water levels; the moon, and insect hatches to name just a few.

Another factor to consider is "fisherman activity." Fifty boats and fifty float-tubes on a 600-acre lake eventually spook trout into inactivity.

The successful fisherman, who seems to catch fish when others fail, invariably is the one who understands that conditions in fish habitat are not static. The underwater world changes frequently and as fishermen, although we can't know all the changes, we must be aware they occur.

What is the single most important characteristic or skill of the really good fisherman? His ability with the fly rod? A knack for reading water? Or general dedication to fishing? In my opinion, "imagination " separates the less effective anglers from the pros. The pro is willing to try anything to catch fish. He better understands what is going on "down under" and is able to adapt his tackle to the various conditions.

I once read an article in which a top tournament bass fisherman told of his concepts of catching more and bigger bass. One part of the article really set me to thinking about lake and reservoir trout fishing. The bass pro said he had a lot of theories but that at the moment he was working most on "wind."

He believed that wind direction is important in fishing shoals and structures and said he kept accurate records that tended to support his theory. Lakes are definitely not as "static" as people think, he maintained. While scuba diving, he had observed grass and sediment moving, much as a stream current moves objects.

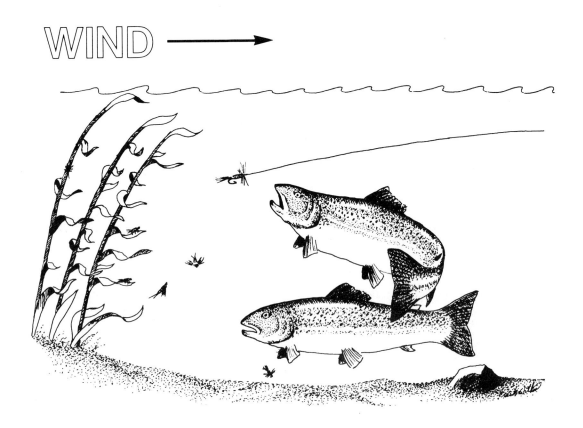

Trout in a stream feed on objects moving downstream. Since most stillwater trout are native to streams, it would seem reasonable to assume they would instinctively look for a downstream movement of food in lakes also. I kept track of my strikes on several trips while fishing downwind as opposed to fishing upwind. It was not a valid "laboratory" experiment, but I did catch more fish casting into the wind working my fly downwind, particularly when fishing structures with weed beds.

I could visualize in my mind the fish lying downwind of the nymph laden weed beds waiting for the waves to wash their dinner to them.

Too much imagination? Consider the following:

For several years I've experienced a fishing phenomenon, which for a time, I dismissed as coincidence. I noticed that when fishing wet flies or nymphs, particularly in lakes and reservoirs, I had more strikes on a fly I had just tied on than on one that had been fished for a time. In talking with other fishermen I confirmed my observations on the phenomenon.

"Coincidence!" you say. "No reason for such a thing to happen."

I'm not so sure. It has happened too many times to be purely coincidental. I spent considerable time on one trip recently, experimenting with different patterns to see if the "phenomenon" held up. On five different occasions, after unsuccessfully fishing a brown leech pattern through some high percentage water, I changed to a fresh copy, and each time I got a strike on the first cast.

For the sake of argument let's assume a fresh fly catches fish more easily then one that has been fished for some time. But why?

The first thing that comes to mind is the possibility that the change in color, from the fly soaking up water, is somehow more attractive to fish as it makes this "color transition." It's a plausible explanation, but not my favorite.

The possibility more in tune to my personal thinking, is that the new fly traps air bubbles and moves naturally through the water, thus appearing more palatable to the fish. Although this might seem a bit far-fetched, it leads to my third hypothesis — the one I believe holds more weight than the others.

Angling author Pete Hidy (co-author with the late Jim Leisenring of "THE ART OF TYING THE WET FLY AND FISHING THE FLYMPH") has given credence to the "flymph" theory of nymphs hatching in a bubble of compressed gas, which is generated in hatching. The flies Pete dresses have dubbed fur bodies and soft hen hackle legs that trap air bubbles mimicking the natural hatching nymph. I see a relationship between the "flymph" theory and my "first-cast theory" and have arrived at several conclusions.

First, I find the theory works more often with mohair or fur-bodied patterns than it does with chenille or hard bodies. The fur or mohair traps air more easily and gives the illusion of the natural nymph.

Second, I find the theory works better when I'm fishing a floating or slow-sinking line. I believe fish are looking for hatching insects, with accompanying gaseous air bubbles, and when the new pattern floats into view they pounce on it.

Third, the flymph theory might explain why mohair patterns are so important to float-tube fishermen. Mohair, particularly the long-strand variety holds more air, and thus would appear more "natural" to fish. Most of us who have fished mohair so religiously thought the translucence of the material attracted fish. It probably is the combination of translucence and trapped air that makes mohair flies so effective.

Being imaginative also can backfire, as it did the day I was searching for trout with the two-fly system.

The dropper technique — using two flies, one at the terminal end of the leader and the other higher up the leader — is not used to any great extent by float-tubers, but is a good method for finding the "hot pattern."

I fasten the dropper fly about three feet above my terminal fly. I double the material at the blood knot and end up with a dropper almost as strong as the main stem. If I don't know for sure what the fish are taking I double my chances with each cast when I'm using the system. But on a trip to Horsethief Reservoir something happened that caused me to have second thoughts about using two flies.

I was tubing near the center of the lake (thankfully by myself) when I had a sharp strike. The rainbow trout broke water in a looping jump, then another, another and another. Now there is nothing out of the ordinary about a rainbow trout jumping, except that each time it broke water it was six feet closer to me. On its final jump the trout bounced off my float-tube and the upper "dropper fly" snagged firmly in my wool shirt.

Since my dropper was tied on at the 10-pound test blood knot, it held firmly and my trout (the best of the trip of course) broke loose and swam off.

The incident recalled an earlier experience in which I also had trouble with my two-fly system.

I had hooked two trout at the same time and netted the bottom fish first. I dropped the fly back in the water and netted the second fish.

I realized in a flash that I had made a serious error. The bottom fly firmly snagged my waders just above my ankle. A fellow float-tuber, Boisean Al Hansen, removed the fly from my waders and swore a blood oath never to tell.

Despite certain hazards of the two-fly system, it is good when searching for fish. But it must be used with caution . . .

Chapter 9

The Retrieve

I once was fishing one of my favorite Central Idaho trout reservoirs and hooking fish on every fourth or fifth cast. I was using a reddish-brown leech pattern (the Canadian Brown), fished on a deep sinking line with a super quick retrieve. I would let my hi-density line sink for a 25-count and then retrieve with 12-inch rips as fast as I could bring it in.

As I netted and released a nice 2-pound rainbow, another tuber moved in and asked to see my fly. I showed it to him and we began to discuss lines and retrieves. My friend was using the same fly — as a matter-of-fact it was one I'd given him an hour earlier — and the same line. When I showed him my retrieve, he admonished me "That's not how you retrieve a leech!" and paddled away.

Being the "hard-head" I am, I continued to retrieve my way and continued to hook fish. My friend fished his fly slowly, the "proper" way to fish a leech, and continued fishless.

The episode demonstrates a common fault in fly fishing stillwater. Don't get locked into one or two retrieves and miss the action because the fish have decided they want their lunch served differently.

The most common float-tube retrieves include:

• The "standard retrieve" of 3-inch rips in rapid succession or about 2 or 3 sec-

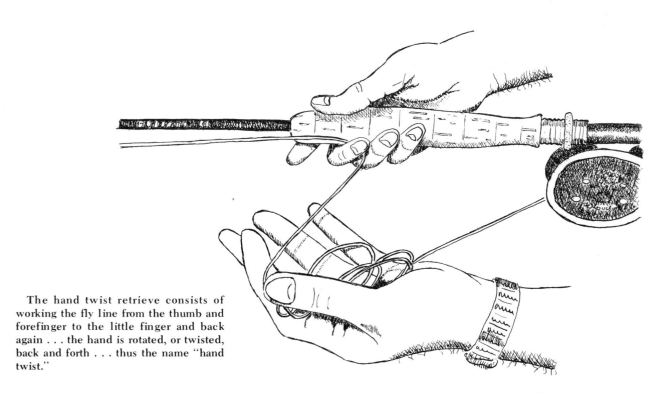

The hand twist retrieve consists of working the fly line from the thumb and forefinger to the little finger and back again . . . the hand is rotated, or twisted, back and forth . . . thus the name "hand twist."

In retrieving the fly line is fed from the stripping guide through the middle finger down to the other hand. The same posture applies when playing fish.

onds apart, usually in groups of three. The standard also can include groups of 8, 15, or 24-inch rips.

• The "varied" retrieve is a sequence of two . . . one . . . two . . . one . . . etc. While the most common is groups of three and eight-inchers, as with the standard it can include 15 and 24-inchers.

• Another effective retrieve is three 8-inch rips interspaced with pauses of 8 to 10 seconds. Again other length rips may be used.

• The "dead drift" is often a good bet when fish aren't moving. In this case the tuber casts, lets his line sink as deep as he thinks proper and trolls it very slowly by gently wiggling his scuba fins.

• The dead drift can be varied with short rips every 15 to 20 seconds. The rips can be of any length.

• The Henry's Lake retrieve, especially effective with shrimp patterns, consists of six or seven very fast 3-inch rips, two or three super fast 8-inch rips with an occasional 15-inch rip. Some of the really good Henry's Lake fly rodders become quite creative with their versions of the "Henry's Rip."

• The "super quick" retrieve that I referred to at the beginning of this chapter consists of 15-inch rips as fast as they can be made. I usually fish this type of retrieve with a hi-density line, right off the bottom.

• A novel retrieve I've had good luck with is one where I cast about 15 feet and "let out" 8-inches of fly line every 10 or 15 seconds, while slowly moving, until I've extended it about 50 feet. I then retrieve with one of the other methods.

• The final retrieve is the basic "hand-twist." It is very effective on western trout lakes, particularly during early or late season.

When fishing gets tough the good tuber will go through these variations of retrieves until, quite often, he finds one even the most stubborn fish can't resist.

50

Chapter 10

Playing Fish

I had a superb instructor teach me float-tube nymph fishing. He knew most of the good tubing spots in the area, dressed his own flies and released 95% of the trout he hooked.

He had two habits, however, I didn't like: he caught more fish than I did, and using a heavy rod, he quickly played his fish to the tube. I used to kid him about his derrick-like equipment and the way he man-handled trout.

I had been something of an "ultra-light" spin-fishing addict and thought it was more sporting to play fish until they were totally worn out. Then I read a piece written by fellow Idahoan Ted Trueblood about using "proper tackle" in playing fish. In a nutshell, what Ted said was that the fisherman should use tackle "heavy enough to bring fish to the net as quickly as possible."

My initial reaction was that Ted finally had written something I could find fault with. How could it be more sporting to hook a three-pound trout on 8-pound test line than on 2-pound. It surely took more skill to play a fish on lighter line, and after all, that is what it's all about.

The hook up . . . (Angler — Ruel Stayner)

Playing the fish . . .

Netting it . . .

The gentle release . . .

Then one day I was tubing a little lake that produces excellent rainbow trout up to three or four pounds. I was using two-pound tippets and landing and releasing one tired out trout after another. The lake was calm and here and there I could see trout near the surface. One particular fish seemed reluctant to move, so I decided to see how close I could tube to the fish. I ended up netting the rainbow, one which I had released earlier.

The fish was not bleeding, and I had previously released it without removing it from the net. I hadn't squeezed it, so I knew there couldn't be internal injuries. I righted the big trout and gently revived it until it swam away . . . hopefully to be caught another day.

I finally realized what Ted had meant when he said we should use "proper tackle" in order to land fish quickly. Any fish we intend to release should be in proper condition to survive. As fishermen, we can contribute to that condition by playing our fish to the net quickly and by being extra gentle to those we release. When we find blood near the gill structure, the fish should be killed immediately, and consumed while fresh.

Some misunderstanding exists among anglers as to the survival rate of released fish. I've heard fishermen suggest that every fly-caught trout dies. They suggest that fly fishermen should "catch their limits" and go home early so others can get their limits.

The best information I can obtain is that properly released trout have approximately a 95 percent survival rate. That is for every 100 trout released, 95 will live. If we are as careful as we can be in releasing trout, we should be able to improve that percentage by at least two or three points.

For the sake of argument, let's assume five out of every hundred released trout do die. Let's take two similar lakes, starting with 20,000 trout in each, and fish one with the "kill" method and the other "catch and release."

If we average 50 anglers on each lake, we come up with the following figures: On the kill lake, assuming our anglers catch a limit of 10 fish per day, they would fish the lake out in 40 days. On the catch and release lake with the same number of fishermen, we will assume each angler lands and releases 20 fish — double the fun of the kill lake. There will be a mortality of 50 fish per day. At the end of 40 days, at which point the "kill" lake is theoretically "fished out," 18,000 fish will remain in the catch and release lake. It would take an additional 360 days to "theoretically" fish the lake out.

On the kill lake our 50 fishermen have enjoyed 40 days catching their 20,000 trout. On the catch-and-release lake our 50 anglers have enjoyed 400 days of fishing, averaging 1,000 fish per day. In the end the original 20,000 fish have been caught and released 400,000 times.

I believe Lee Wulff said it best when he was quoted, "A trout is too valuable to be caught only once."

A fine brown trout will live to fight another day.

Chapter 11

High Lakes and Float Tubes

Overwhelming frustration can come to sportsmen in many ways.
A bird-hunter is working a brace of dogs in an Idaho sugarbeet field. The dogs set and flush a trio of rooster pheasants and the Parker clicks on empty chambers.

An elk hunter tracks a herd in deep snow — in a bulls only area — and after long hours walks up to a group of twenty cows and calves.

These are examples of genuine frustration. But if I had to pick my most frustrating outdoors experience, it would be something that happened to me on one of Idaho's finest high mountain lakes. The scene: Ten acres of lovely emerald-green water, liberally laced with high-country moss beds and dotted with lily-pads. The sun is setting and a smuttering rise of diptera stimulates a good population of rainbow trout into frenzied feeding.

Three- to four-pound fish begin cruising the shoreline, feeding at predictable intervals on the tiny emerging midge. I pick a strategic casting station. A peninsula from which I can cast to rising fish in three different directions. Using a 7X tippet, I deftly drop size 22 and 24 dry flies and pupas to the feeding fish.

I cast . . . and cast . . . and cast. Four-pounders feed to my right . . . and four-pounders feed to my left. I cast . . . and cast . . . and cast.

Ninety minutes later, I am completely wilted, drenched with perspiration, fishless, and . . . completely frustrated. I've had two such experiences on the little mountain lake. I'm not sure I could stand a third.

"Side benefits" do result from such experiences. At least that's what it says in the *Sportsman's Handbook* . . . in very fine print. Besides making occasional moments of success sweeter, "frustrations" tend to deflate super-egos and provide tons and tons of humility.

The major problem a fly fisherman encounters in fishing high lakes, is how to make a decent back-cast. It isn't often we find a casting station, such as the one described above, that allows for easy back-casts.

Since many high lakes require hikes of several miles it is not always practical to carry a boat. Sometimes we find log rafts, or are able to build one, allowing some degree of mobility. But if you haven't fished from a crudely built log raft, a unique experience awaits you.

The first such raft I used was on Honeymoon Lake, a beautiful jewel of a lake near the Central Idaho Primitive Area. Honeymoon had a reputation for producing rainbows in the seven- or eight-pound range so I felt lucky when I located a reasonably seaworthy log raft along the shallow end of the lake. I was trolling a renegade dry fly, exploring the fringe of the little lake, when a large trout decided my fly was the best looking meal he'd seen in weeks.

The fish grabbed my fly and my untended rod went over the end of the raft and began to sink. Since it was the only equipment I had carried in, I had only a second or two to make up my mind. I didn't hesitate. Diving over the side I managed to grab the sinking rod at a depth of six or seven feet.

Float-tubes and high lakes are a good combination.

The fish was long gone, but at that point I wasn't concerned with landing a fish. I swam to the raft and discovered my problems had only began. The raft's logs were covered with a thick layer of slime. I could get a fairly good grip on the platform, but I needed to swing my knees up in order to climb abroad. I mentally compared my predicament with climbing a "greased pole."

I ended up towing the raft to shore.

From that day, I have carefully cleaned the slime off any high lake raft I use. Although I've caught some nice trout in several Idaho and Montana high lakes, I believe the Honeymoon Lake fish I lost might have been the biggest of all.

The float-tube may not have been designed with high lakes in mind, but it should have been. It can be deflated, stowed comfortably aboard a pack horse or personal pack-board and carried with comparative ease. It is easily inflated with a simple tire pump.

In fishing high lakes before I became a float-tuber, I had always used tiny dry flies, Mepps-type spinners or salmon eggs. Once I learned something about tube fishing nymphs and began tying flies, I changed my thinking about mountain lakes. I discovered that in addition to taking high country trout on small flies, I also could catch them on many of our lowland reservoir patterns.

The entomology of a high lake is more similar to desert reservoirs than I had believed. Almost all high country lakes contain populations of dragonflies, damsel flies, leeches and shrimp. It may offend some high lake purists who insist on fishing

56

A beautiful high lake rainbow trout about to be released.

with 7X tippets and 24 dries — but the deep sinking line with heavy dragonfly nymphs will take fish. In many cases the larger fish.

The only real difference between fishing crystal-clear alpine lakes and lower reservoirs, is the length of the leader and the length of the cast. I fish high lakes as if I were fishing a spring creek. I lengthen my leader to 15 feet and work with a long distance casting technique.

Day in and day out, lowland reservoirs may produce larger trout than high mountain lakes, but not larger rewards. The contentment a float-tuber can find floating around in a crystal-clear high mountain lake will more than balance the scale.

Chapter 12

The Last Trout In The River: An Essay

Mutuk moved swiftly from his lair to inspect the morsel drifting by and quickly rejected it.

Mutuk was hungry, but he still had the caution that had contributed to his great age. Drifting back beneath his log, Mutuk gently moved his giant caudal fin and continued to watch his feeding lane.

Mutuk could see the "little ones" scurrying among the rocks. His hunger drive was so strong that he considered foraging among his smaller counterparts. But vivid memories of earlier years restrained him.

Mutuk had felt the "tightness" in his greed for the little ones. The first time had frightened Mutuk for only a fleeting moment. He had rid himself of the tightness by moving into the forest of roots next to his lair.

But the second time gave Mutuk everlasting caution regarding the little ones. The tightness caused by the second imitation little one had been much deeper in his throat. He had tried to move into his root forest but the pressure from the outsider had been too much. Mutuk had been forced from the security of his lair into the deeper part of his world. Mutuk had jumped headlong into the outside world twice before he finally felt the pressure in his throat relax.

The imitation little one still stuck in Mutuk's throat but he was no longer controlled by the outsider. It was many darknesses before the "thing" loosened its grip and fell from Mutuk's giant jaws.

Mutuk watched his feeding lane for periods of time without seeing any food. Although Mutuk's intelligence was limited to basic drives, he was aware that the foodless periods were longer than in the past. Mutuk was concerned about this problem, but he was aware of an even more dangerous situation. Mutuk's world was growing smaller and smaller with every darkness.

He could sense a much different "feeling" in his world, Mutuk was having a difficult time keeping his senses. More and more he felt the need to drift to the surface and gulp the freshness of the outside world. Since the preceding darkness Mutuk had felt his world diminish almost to the size of his safety log. He was beginning to have the same fear as when the imitation little ones had stuck in his jaw.

Mutuk also was aware that more and more outsiders were invading his world. Recently he had been forced to retreat twice into the deepest part of his world only to find the outsiders still in pursuit.

Mutuk was growing weary of the game. Food was scarce, his safety threatened. He knew he had to make a decision. He could remain in his lair and end up being scooped up by the outsiders. Or he could move upstream in search of a safer lair and hope to avoid the hunters. His intelligence didn't warn him of the consequences of leaving his safety.

He moved as darkness set in, it was safer that way. He knew the outsiders didn't hunt in the darkness, and his world was more comfortable. Mutuk moved through three darknesses before he discovered how fruitless his endeavor was. A giant obstruction had been placed across his beloved world. He could go no further.

Mutuk rested through a complete darkness and reasoned he must return to his home lair. It was difficult to find his direction, freshness no longer came from above. His world no longer moved. Mutuk circled the pool several times before he realized there was no way out. He would have to wait for a new freshness from above before he could go back to his lair.

He waited and waited. He had no way of knowing how long his wait might be. After the fourth darkness, the outsiders again came. This time they didn't use imitation little ones. They used a thing that reminded Mutuk of his forest of roots. But Mutuk couldn't move through it. He was trapped by the web-like tangle.

Mutuk was panicked as outsiders lifted him from his world. It was only a momentary panic. Mutuk felt a sense of relief. He had greatly surpassed life expectancy and had out lived all others of his race. He was the last survivor.

The outsiders won the final battle, not with the little ones but with another weapon. They had turned off Mutuk's world with the "giant obstruction."

Mutuk accepted defeat as part of his life. With his death, the outsiders also tasted defeat. It too was becoming part of their life.

Mutuk wondered who the winners were?

PART III
THE FISH

Chapter 13

Rainbow Trout

The day ended much as it had begun. Over-sized raindrops beat a steady tattoo against our tent walls, exploding like tiny bombs in some crazy, miniature war.

The shrill grunting bugle of a lonesome bull elk in a meadow across the lake blended eerily with the twilight. Overhead, the ponderosa pines that towered above our camp wore a misty halo, their branches drooping heavily from three days of rain.

The wind, which at midday had riffled the lake threateningly now was so quiet that the flutter of a camp robber's wings seemed somehow ominous.

A line from Longfellow described the scene perfectly: "The murmuring of the pines and the hemlocks, bearded with moss and in garments green, indistinct in the twilight, stand like druids of eld." If druidism "was" tree-worship, I could almost believe it was omens like this that brought the ancient Celts of Gaul into the woods on bended knee.

The chill of the early September evening added to my frustrating battle to rekindle a stubborn campfire. A pot of sheepherder coffee waiting glumly alongside our grill seemed impatient with my wet, clumsy efforts.

I had just won the campfire battle when Dad returned with a trio of fat two-

Phil Anderson of Boise with a very "cooperative" rainbow trout.

pound rainbows. Never one to miss an opportunity in our running competition on who was the better angler, Dad chided me, "you and your 'renegades' are great for minnows but do you know what pattern I caught these beauties on?"

"The Velvetta special?"

"How'd you guess?"

"Just a hunch," I said, hoping to end the conversation. It didn't. Dad reminisced on the fishing we had known at Sage Hen Reservoir in earlier years and continued to needle me about having given up my standby baits in favor of artificials.

The sizzle of trout and pan-fried potatoes soon took Dad's mind off my inadequacies with the fly rod, and we were enjoying an evening meal that could be accurately described only in the consumption. Although we ate that meal many years ago, I remember it as clearly as yesterday.

That weekend trip wasn't my first experience with the fly rod — I took my first trout, a brookie, on a fly when I was nine years old — but it was the first time I consciously fished "nymphs."

While Dad used bait for most of the four days we fished, I caught all of my trout on either a mosquito or renegade dry fly fished "wet." As I look back on the trip, I remember some pretty good caddis and midge hatches. My guess is that the trout took my No. 14 mosquito for midge pupas, and my reneade for emerging caddis flies.

I bought my first sinking fly line that same year, 1962 — while on a trip to Montana — and an evolution began that finally put me in a float-tube in 1969. Al-

though I've come to appreciate all of our trout, particularly the brown, my first love is the rainbow trout.

I hold the "bow" in such esteem for three basic reasons. First, they are the most spectacular to catch. Show me a fisherman who won't admit to being thrilled by a leaping trout, and I'll show you one who wouldn't praise motherhood or apple pie. Secondly, rainbows are native to the Northwest. I was raised with these beautiful red-sided salmonoids and as good as some of the other species might be, my first love has been my strongest love.

My third reason for appreciating rainbow trout is perhaps the most rational reason of all . . . at least for a dyed-in-the-wool fly fisherman. Rainbows are probably — with the possible exception of brook trout — the dumbest and easiest to fool of all fish. They will eat anything . . . and everything. I've caught them on just about every known fly pattern and a few hundred that aren't "known."

Rainbows' feeding patterns are longer than cutthroat or brown trout. They often will feed from sunup to sundown. Although I find I'm writing more in my fishing column about "smelling the roses," I still like to catch fish.

The rainbow obliges me more frequently than any other fish.

Chapter 14

Cutthroat Trout

I caught my first cutthroat in one of Idaho's mountain lakes. It was ten-inches long and just about the prettiest fish I had ever seen. I was only 12 years old and totally overwhelmed by the beauty of the back country and the willingness of the little cutthroat to bite my hook. I don't remember the name of the lake, nor the bait I was using, but I do remember I was hooked on stillwater trout fishing.

Cutthroat also are native to the Northwest and near and dear to the hearts of most fly fishermen. They often are a most willing victim for a fly fisherman. They can be taken on just about any fly pattern in the book as they are more often "insect-eaters" than "meat-eaters."

While sea-run cutthroat attract lots of attention, the high country cuts and "big-impoundment fish" set this species apart. Within what I call the "magic-thousand-mile" circle, lies some of the best float-tube fly fishing in the world. The best of the best includes such cutthroat fisheries as Pyramid Lake in Nevada, Henry's in Idaho, and, of course, Yellowstone Lake in Wyoming.

But for an angler who wants solitude along with his trout fishing, something you unfortunately can't get at Pyramid, Henry's or Yellowstone, the high lakes offer the float-tuber something more than gigantic trout.

The things we remember best about a fishing trip often are not the fish we bag. As good or bad as the fishing may be, usually it's another aspect of the trip we recall best. Little things make the difference.

The aroma of bacon frying in the thin, high country air.

The first rays of the morning sun, casting shadows that dance across the face of a bluff above a lake.

The cool breeze drying your hard-earned perspiration as you top that last ridge on the hike in.

The shy doe with twin fawns crossing the trail near timberline and the pair of blue jays that bounce from limb to limb in the gnarled, centuries old spruce.

The absolute stillness of the high country, punctuated by the awesome sounds of an August thunderstorm.

The pounding impact of raindrops against a hurriedly constructed shelter. The subtle quiet as the rain turns to sleet and then snow.

The gentleness of a snowflake falling as you hear the soft splash of the day's first feeding trout.

The joy of the first cast and the electricity of the strike.

The contentment of a high country cutthroat lake.

Chapter 15

Brook Trout

I once was asked to list my choices for: the easiest lake from which to catch big trout; the most difficult; the one that requires the most concentration; and my favorite.

My answer to all four questions came in two words: Henry's Lake.

Located in eastern Idaho near the entrance to Yellowstone Park, Henry's can be an exciting lake for the fly fisherman. It not only has "lots" of trout (rainbow-cutthroat hybrids, cutthroat and brook trout) but lots of "big" trout.

When I think about Henry's Lake I recall a day in 1976 that vividly describes the "appreciative" attitude most fly fishermen have of the lake.

The day began as one of those superb eastern Idaho high country mornings. The sun broke over the ridge at Targhee Pass and seemed to shower us with a promise of things to come. The lake was calm, only the soft splash of fishing line hitting water and an occasional, "I missed him!" could be heard.

I was particularly relaxed and completely at peace with the world that morning. The joy of just "wetting a line" was partly responsible for my state of mind. The four-pound brook trout I had taken the previous day also may have had something to do with it.

Fishing had been sporadic all morning. We had caught a few fish before sunup but the action had been all too brief. Mostly we were sitting in our tubes, soaking up atmosphere and waiting for the morning damsel hatch.

My fishing partners and I were passing the time by practicing our casting. I had just completed a decent cast when one of my buddies caught my eye and motioned up the lake, "He's onto a good one."

The three of us sat and watched another of our friends play out what appeared to be an especially heavy trout. Since we were a couple of hundred yards away we couldn't see the size of the fish when he put it on his stringer. I knew he had received orders to bring home a couple of "smokers" so I guessed he had a big one when he immediately began tubing towards shore.

We made another cast, but then one of the anglers looked back at his trailer, and quickly gathered up his line. "That fish I gotta see," he grunted.

My remaining companion and I continued to practice our casting techniques without disturbing any of the sleeping fish.

After about a half hour I was jolted out of semi-slumber by a voice from the shoreline. "Hey Marv," he shouted, "you got a scale that goes over twelve pounds?" I looked over at my companion, he shrugged "no" — so I told our buddies on shore that not having caught many trout over twelve pounds I hadn't seen any reason for such a large de-liar.

When the two men on shore wandered back to their trailer I looked over at my companion, nodding my head toward the trailer. He grinned agreement to my non-verbalized question. We stopped at my camper, picked up a pair of cameras and attempted to be casual as we wandered up to the trailer.

As we neared, I noticed a pair of 3-pound cutthroat lying in the shade. In the trailer our fishing partners were frying bacon and eggs.

"Where's the big one?" I asked, eager to take pictures. I had barely spoken when the "light" began to dawn. Not knowing when to give up I blundered on. "The big fish, the one you needed a twelve pound scale for."

"Now Marv," our partner drawled. "We didn't say we had a big fish. We only asked if you had a scale that went over twelve-pounds."

At that point the joke became painfully obvious. What appeared to be one big fish, had been two. I stood there with two cameras around my neck and attempted, with little success, to blend into the background.

Few places on the North American continent would engender this type of prank. The "possibility" of super-big fish must exist for such a charade. Henry's Lake has fish worthy of fantasy.

While many fishermen hope to catch one of Henry's famous ten-pound "hybrids," a trophy brook trout is the most coveted prize.

Fishing Henry's Lake in July and August, when most of the fishing activity occurs, is limited mainly to the fly rod. Trolling usually ends by July 4th because of extensive weed growth.

To catch brook trout in Henry's Lake, you first must understand that this species prefers colder water than much of the shallow lake can provide during the summer months. You must fish near springs and at the mouths of creeks. Staley Springs, Duck Creek, Hope Creek and Howard Creek are popular spots.

You learn the weed beds and how deep the water is at each spot. You learn how long it takes your fast sinking fly line to reach bottom. A good place to begin is forty-five seconds with a medium-fast sinking line. If you pull up weeds, subtract seconds, if you don't, add seconds.

If you are to be successful you also learn the Henry's Lake fly-pattern rotation. You begin the day at 5 A.M. with your favorite version of a Henry's Lake Leech. If your retrieve is right and the fish cooperative, you can stay with it until 8 or 9 A.M.

When the leech no longer produces, you switch to the shrimp pattern. While

The author with a four-pound Henry's Lake brook trout.

there are a number of good variations, I prefer the skunk. It is dressed with fluorescent green chenille with a black strip down the back. The shrimp can be good most of the day unless the damsels are hatching. In that event you try and come up with a damsel imitation the fish will accept. The damsel nymph pattern usually will catch fish until about 5 P.M.

Evening fishing can be the toughest at Henry's. I've had shrimp patterns and coon bugs do well from 6 until 9 P.M. The leech usually will begin working again about 8:30 P.M.

Each pattern is fished differently. The leech is worked rather slowly, beginning right on the bottom. The shrimp retrieve is a series of very short, quick rips. Again . . . right off the bottom.

The damsel nymph is worked in an in-between fashion.

Other patterns also work. Woolly worms produce well at times, and each flytier has a pet or two that have been "one-day killers."

But just having the right fly, right line and right retrieve, isn't always enough on Henry's Lake. You think you have it all figured out, and then a couple of guys from Tremonton, Utah; or my friend Hal Janssen from California will come along and rip fish out on every cast while you sit in your tube flailing the water to a froth without so much as a bump.

They'll tell you the line they are using and even give you their fly patterns. They'll give you all kinds of advice . . . all to no avail. That's when you learn to "hate" Henry's Lake.

But you'll go back. Again . . . and again . . . and again. One fine day it's you sitting out there catching all the fish . . . ringed by fishless boats, filled with anglers talking to themselves. At this point, the ever unpredictable Henry's Lake once again is your favorite fishing hole.

Chapter 16

Brown Trout

The brown trout is quasi-native in many parts of the west, but not in Idaho. Fishery managers in Idaho for many years considered the brown an undesirable alien and stocked the fish only in a few streams. According to some stories, many early brown trout plants were actually made by private citizens.

This dogmatic attitude towards the brown trout has changed in recent years. Fly fishermen hail the change. Besides being a great sport-fish — to all fishermen regardless of their choice of tackle — the brown trout, due partly to his nocturnal nature, seems to grow larger, offering the trophy angler a better chance for success.

My initial experience with brown trout was on the Big Hole River in Montana. I had read an article by the late Joe Brooks about the Big Hole browns, and since my work took me to Butte, I decided to spend some time on the river.

I was fishing a stretch just upstream from Twin Bridges, catching lots of small rainbow but no brown trout. As I landed and released a 12-inch rainbow I noticed a large "carp" boil the surface across the river. I remember feeling cheated that I'd come to such a classic trout river only to face the possibility that my largest fish might be one of the carp I'd seen working the surface.

Another fly fisherman, working his way downstream stopped and we discussed the day's fishing. When I mentioned the carp the other angler grinned and asked where I'd seen them. I pointed to the spot I'd last seen one of the big yellow fish, telling my new friend to go ahead and cast.

Using a marabou muddler — at the time I didn't know what marabou was — the other fly fisherman hooked a heavy fish on his first cast. It turned out to be a four-pound brown. On his next cast he hooked and lost an even larger fish. Before his third cast I was on my way to Twin Bridges to buy some marabou muddlers.

Although the brown trout is well established in much of the west it isn't necessarily the float-tuber's first choice. Rainbows, cutthroat and brook trout are easier to find and much easier to catch.

But if I had to stake my life on catching a five-pound trout in one day of fishing, I'd head for someplace like Montana's Clark Canyon Reservoir or Oregon's East Lake.

I'd launch my tube near an inlet stream where I'd likely find good numbers of forage fish and I'd fish streamer patterns like the marabou muddler or leech patterns. I'd fish as late in the evening as practical or legal, and I'd fish hard. On the average day I'm fairly confident I would take a fish in the five-pound range.

The typical brown trout is olive to golden brown in color with large brown or black spots on its sides, back and dorsal fin. The spots usually are surrounded by faint halos of a lighter shade than the body. A lesser number of red or orange spots sometimes are evident along the lateral surface; the dorsal and adipose fins often are fringed or spotted with bright orange or red.

At one time two distinct wild strains of brown trout existed in the United States; the Van Behr or German brown trout, and the Loch Leven or Scottish strain. The former has both red and black spots while the Loch Leven is entirely spotted in black.

Chapter 17

Bluegill

Being completely "single-minded" about any aspect of fishing or hunting, provides both danger and security. The "security" of a positive, single-minded attitude stagnates a normally inquisitive mind. If you know it all, you don't have to explore any "new" horizons.

The "danger" of being a "know-it-all hard-head" is that others might do something better, more quickly or more completely than you do, simply because you are too stubborn to admit there might be a better way.

But the greatest hazard facing the sportsman who suffers these symptoms is boxing himself into a corner from which he might someday have to extricate himself.

Some years ago, I told a fishing buddy who was praising the largemouth bass as better table fare than trout, that "I'd as soon eat fried grasshoppers as either bass or crappie." Later when I found out you don't "fry" spiney rays like trout, but rather they should be deep-fat fried, I discovered he was right. Bass, bluegill and crappies "are" better eating than trout.

I also had a somewhat "narrow" view regarding bluegill fishing. I associated it with kids in straw hats and sneakers, using willow poles, bobbers and angle worms. My enlightenment took place several years ago at one of Idaho's fine bluegill ponds, Bruneau Sand Dune State Park. I've come to admire the little panfish as something quite special and spend considerable time each spring pursuing them with almost religious fervor. I get as much pleasure with my fly rod and float-tube, fishing for bluegill at the Dunes as I do fishing for lunker brook trout at Henry's Lake.

If you were to try and compare fly fishing for bluegill to fly fishing for bone-fish or tarpon you would be disappointed. But since fishing is relative — the tackle differs for every species of fish — such a comparision can't be made fairly.

The first draft of this chapter described the smashing attacks bluegills make on a surface popper or hair-bug and an account of my monumental battle, which I eventually lost, with a bull bluegill that I believe would have gone well over two pounds. But as I was about to type my final draft, a thought struck me. Although they are rated pound for pound near the top as a fresh water sport fish, it isn't the bluegills' fighting ability that attracts fishermen, it's the fact that anglers can go to their favorite bream pond and catch fish . . . lots of fish . . . almost anytime.

And eating these fish really sews it up. Most piscatorial gourmets rate bluegill as one of the finest eating fresh water fish.

Most fishermen with whom I have talked have never caught a bluegill. This doesn't surprise me because until eight or nine years ago I hadn't either. Since being exposed to the little sunfish I have studied its life style intensively. (I call it scientific research. My wife says I just fish a lot.)

The bluegill is not native to Idaho. It was planted in some farm ponds many years ago by sportsmen and farmers interested in better utilizing stock watering and irrigation ponds.

Bluegill are susceptible to all types of gear and bait. The spin fisherman uses small spinners, spoons and jigs. The fly rodder goes with poppers, dry flies, stream-

Boisean Pat Pennie, a spring bluegill pond, and the beginning of a fish dinner.

ers and nymphs. Bait fishermen generally use bobbers and worms. When the fish are feeding, no special technique is required.

I've watched children as young as four or five screech with delight over a bluegill on the end of their line. I've watched seniors, no longer able to wade trout streams, having the time of their lives on a good bluegill pond.

Bluegill fishing also is a excellent way to learn float-tube fly fishing.

Fly fishermen generally begin the bluegill season with nymphs and sinking lines. Fom my experience, both fishing and talking with other fishermen I recommend beginning with one of the peacock-body nymphs — the Zug Bug and Prince Nymph are examples — and fishing it very slowly. Unless bluegill are on their spawning beds, they will not follow a fly very far. The most common fault among unsuccessful bluegill fly fishermen is that they "rush" the fly.

When bluegill move to the spawning beds, knowledgeable fly fishermen will change to a floating line and use poppers, hair bugs or spiders. Unless you have seen a bluegill strike a surface lure you cannot believe the power generated by such a small body.

Spawning takes place when water temperatures reach 70 to 75 degrees. Since spawning beds usually are located in fairly shallow water, you can often reach them from the bank. I find the float-tube, however, to be the perfect technique for finding and catching bluegill on most lakes and ponds. The tube is more mobile than a boat — particularly in smaller ponds — easier to cast from in windy conditions and more fun. When you are down at "water-zero" you are playing the bream on his terms. When he turns his "dish-shaped" body sideways and stubbornly refuses to yield . . . it's hard not to fall in love with the little critter.

A few years ago, I had a good day on bluegills and was busy filleting a pile of half-pounders when some folks came by to watch. They were interested in my technique with the fillet knife, but apparently not too impressed by the fish.

As the people walked away, I overheard one of the men say, "I really don't know why anyone would get so excited over such small fish. They aren't really worth the effort."

If only that man could join me for just one day at my favorite bream pond. If he could watch as I drop a rubber spider next to a tule bed and sense the anticipation as I wait for the strike I know is coming; if he could breathe the fresh air; soak in the sunshine; absorb the contentment; he might just change his mind about bluegill.

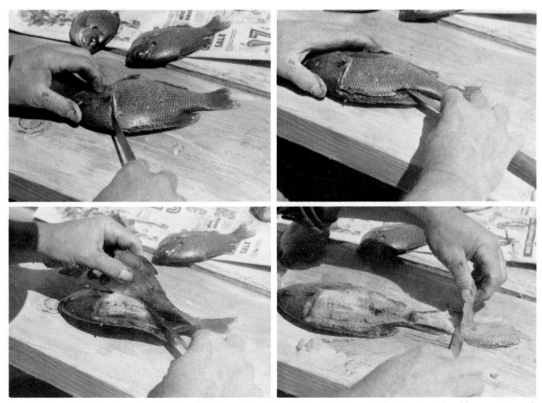

Series of photos showing fillet method — (1) cut behind gill. (2) work knife along backbone. (3) work ribs loose. (4) lay fillet over and separate skin and flesh.

Chapter 18

Largemouth Bass

The big bass was lazily fanning the water just above a sunken log. I had tubed too close to the fish to be able to make a cast without spooking it. The largemouth was only a couple of feet beneath the surface of the "gin-clear" water, and it was easy to make an estimate of it's size. I was sure it would go at least six pounds.

I tried to back off without disturbing the fish; but the sudden movement of my scuba fins broke the spell, and the bass disappeared into the depths of the lake. Since bull bass usually frequent the same area I made a mental note to come back that evening and be a bit more subtle.

The screech of an osprey diverted my attention from the big bass. The fish hawk was circling just overhead, and for a moment I thought he might have designs on me. If he did, he had second thoughts and flew off to his nest atop a dead snag at the far end of the lake.

I watched the big bird land and when I saw a head raise up out of the nest my imagination suggested "mama osprey" was asking "papa osprey" where breakfast was.

"How's fishing?"

The voice broke the magic of the moment and brought me rudely back to reality. On shore was a lone fisherman, clad in the garments of our sport . . . fishing vest, chest high waders, battered felt hat, with a pipe in one hand and a fly rod in the other. For an instant I thought he was a character out of the columns of the late Robert Ruark. The fisherman looked as if he was part of the lake.

We chatted about the fishing, the weather and the lake for a few pleasant moments, and then my new friend, spotting a bass boil the surface down the shoreline, departed as quickly as he had appeared.

I looked back at the sunken log, realizing that the big bass was probably too spooked to strike, made a cast anyway. I let the big bucktail settle just about to the bottom and began a quick, jerky retrieve.

"Wow!" I said under my breath as I felt the jarring strike of a good fish. I said another "Wow!" as the fish bore straight back toward the log. I wish I could report that I landed a fine six-pound largemouth bass. The truth of the matter is that the fish nonchalantly swam under the log, broke me off and casually swam away.

Are giant largemouth merely a fly rodder's fantasy? Are we kidding ourselves when, armed only with a slender, whippy rod, we tackle the bruisers that "hawgmasters" use "telephone poles" on?

Not really. We do have our work cut out for us, but the fantasy of the six-pound bigmouth on a 4-ounce fly rod "is" a possibility. Particularly for the float-tube fly fisherman. The tuber's ability to "penetrate" areas more quietly and stealthily is the advantage a fly rodder has over "bass-stick" proponents. Tubers also can "launch" on smaller ponds than bass boaters.

Although the ubiquitous largemouth does his best to keep his oversized mouth and appetite filled, he is an enigma to the fly rodder. As with the smallmouth we

catch fish, but seldom the really big fish. Our problem with the largemouth is different than with the smallmouth. With the latter it is a matter of getting our fly "deep"
enough. With the largemouth it's getting it "big" enough.

In general, largemouths are "pond fish" and smallmouths are "stream" fish, although they do overlap. A better explanation of their habitats would be that smallmouth prefer colder, cleaner water than largemouth. The largemouth probably can
survive conditions that smallmouth would find completely inhospitable.

Smallmouth prefer to live in deeper water but the largemouth has no scruples
about spending much of his time in fairly shallow water. If there's a fallen log,
rotting tree stump or bunch of lily pads around, odds are good that a largemouth or
two will be hiding in the vicinity, usually out of the direct rays of the sun.

After you've found the bass, how do you catch him? Bait-casters and spin fishermen use floating-diving plugs, lizard type lures and plastic worm — often as large as
10 inches. A quick retrieve allows the angler to cover a great deal of water.

Fly fishermen must attempt to dress their flies in a manner that suggest something big and good to eat. With an appetite the size of a largemouth's it is obvious he
would have to consume a multitude of one-inch minnows to satisfy it. The bass is no
dummy. If he is going to expend energy catching something, it's going to be a
mouthful.

Two of the best fly patterns for largemouth are the "marabou mess" and "serpentine" streamer. The "mess" consists of bountiful fluffs of marabou for wing and tail and a chenille body. It should be weighted with heavy fuse wire before tying. The best colors are solid black, purple or reddish-brown.

The serpentine is tied with four or six, long saddle hackles for a tail and tightly palmered hackles on the bare hook shank for a body. The best colors for the serpentine (in order of importance) are: purple, black and grizzly.

When largemouth are working the surface, cork poppers, or deer-hair bugs will take fish. This type of fishing is usually best during late evening or complete darkness.

Float-tubers going for largemouth bass use considerably heavier tackle than for other spiney rays. He needs at least No. 8 or No. 9 lines to handle the larger weighted flies, poppers and hair-bugs. My favorite bigmouth rod is an 8½-foot graphite weighing about 4½-ounces, which, although rated for No. 8 or No. 9 lines will comfortably handle number 10 steelhead shooting heads. I recommend the beginner buy "bass shooting tapers" in the best quality he can afford.

The formula for success in largemouth bass fly fishing is: fish the largest pattern you can comfortably handle, in or near cover during daylight hours and something big and noisy after the sun sets.

Chapter 19

Smallmouth Bass

The fishing report read: " 'Hawg' smallmouths by the dozens." All you had to do was to run your boat down to Brownlee Reservoir on the Idaho-Oregon border, pick a rocky point and heave in a lure . . . any lure.

I tried it and caught fish. But when you're after "grandpa" and "grandma" and all you catch are 10-inch juveniles, well, you gotta figure you did something wrong.

I wasn't the only one who failed to find big fish. Judging from the long faces at the boat dock when I pulled in the first evening, I had lots of company.

But one angler, a fellow from Portland, hoisted a stringer of three- and four-pound smallmouths that elicited "oh's" and "ah's" all along the dock. The promise of a cup of coffee — liberally laced with some good "Canadian" — enticed the Portland bass fisherman to join Vina and I in our camper. After the normal pleasantries, the bass expert got down to business.

"Your mistake," he said, "might have been the common belief that smallmouths and rocky terrain go together like strawberry shortcake and whipped cream. Might be true," he continued, "for the yearlings, but the heavyweights spend most of their lives ignoring the rocks in favor of relatively clean bottoms."

My new-found friend said he believed most big smallmouths die in eight or ten years and are never seen by fishermen because the places that appeal to the bass don't look very "fishy."

"Ignore your normal impluses," he said, "and fish the areas that others skip. If you're fishing a man-made lake, look for the area that might have been a flooded farm. Leave the rocky points for the other fishermen."

My friend, a perennial Brownlee angler, said he takes his trophy bronzebacks at the same place every year. Big smallmouths, he thinks, live most of the time right on the bottom. They don't migrate, except during spawning runs.

Crayfish, the mainstay of the smallmouth's diet, live on the bottom, so that's where the big ones will be, he reasoned.

"In fact," he said, "you should concentrate your fishing efforts in waters that are rich in crayfish, because scientists have documented that smallmouths grow faster eating these crustaceans than any other food."

Most local anglers have determined that crayfish are the bait of choice. Spin fishermen have a decided advantage over fly fishermen in deep water. Using weighted jigs they can fish in 40 or 50 feet of water where fly fishermen can't reach.

"The best bait for the spin fisherman can be summed up in three words," he said, "jig and eel." He described the best way to fish the lure. "Cast into a bank or along a sloping point and tight-line the lure immediately. That is, recover any slack line and maintain a taut line as the lure drops. Watch it closely and if it stops before it hits bottom, set the hook.

"If the lure hits bottom without a strike let it rest for a moment, and then lift it off slowly and smoothly by raising the rod tip slightly.

"If you're determined to take a trophy bronzeback on a fly, early spring would be the time to do it," he said. "But Brownlee Reservoir is probably not the place to do it.

"The banks are too clean," he said. "Unless there is tight cover on a bank, big smallmouth will remain in water too deep for your fly."

This chat took place several years ago, and I have confirmed much of the Portland bass expert's advice through subsequent experience.

Since most smallmouth habitat in my area consists of rivers or large reservoirs, the bulk of my tubing activity for bass is in search of largemouth. When I do tube for smallmouths on such waters as Anderson Ranch Reservoir or Brownlee Reservoir I fish in much the same manner as for rainbow or brown trout.

My best patterns are minnow imitations such as the Stayner Ducktail, black or reddish brown fluff-butts and crayfish patterns.

Chapter 20

Crappie

My father was a completely dedicated angler. He could sit out a weekend on a sturgeon setline without so much as a nibble and be happy he "got to go fishing."

I think Dad knew our valley's brown bullhead population as well as anyone. He could skin and clean bullheads with speed and skill few other anglers could match. Catfish graced the Taylor table regularly when I was a boy.

But . . . I don't ever remember eating any of the spiney rays we caught. When it came to disposing of our catches of bass and crappie it was always: "They're too hard to clean," or "They aren't worth the effort." Consequently, we gave away every crappie or bass we ever caught.

I was amused to learn in reading a Ted Trueblood column several years ago, that even the "Sage of Owyhee Reservoir" was at one time a "non-believer." In replying to a friend's remark that "crappies are the greatest eating fish there is," Ted answered, "I'd as soon eat an old boot as a crappie."

Since Ted now considers crappies a delicacy — "comparable to shrimp or oysters" — Ted thinks the "boot statement" may be the funniest thing he ever said.

The Taylors also have reached the "delicacy conclusion," regarding crappie, bluegill and "spring bass."

The first step toward total appreciation of spiney rays is to properly clean them. While many methods are acceptable, I prefer filleting. This should be done as soon as possible, with the fillets packed in plastic bags and quickly iced down.

How crappie are cooked is the key to complete enjoyment of the fish. Fillets should be brought to room temperature and salted lightly. While numerous "fancy-batter" recipes are available, we prefer Ted's. First you whip up several eggs, yolks and whites together, and dip the fillets. Then roll them in saltine cracker crumbs and cook very quickly, in hot (375 to 400 degrees) deep fat. Salad oil is Ted's choice for cooking fat.

Trueblood makes a point of cooking only five or six fillets at a time. Too many, he says, cools the oil. Two minutes is about right for a half-pound fish.

Properly done, the fillets are golden brown and crisp on the outside and moist inside. Over-cooking is the worst and most common problem.

Float-tube fly fishing for crappie can be about the fastest fishing I know of. All the angler needs to do is find a crappie bed, tie on a marabou-chenille pattern and "cast." The fish do the rest.

The best time of year for the float-tuber is April and May when crappies are moving to their spawning beds. I remember a trip when we found large males just beginning to "bed." Four of us took 12-inch crappie on every cast for four days. I thought I had the "hot" pattern with a white "fluff butt." But another fellow did equally well on black . . . another on red . . . and another on blue.

I guess the best advice I can offer for crappie fishing is don't complicate it: "when they're hot they're hot, when they're not they're not."

Chapter 21

Old Toothless: An Essay

One of my friends seems to be able to catch fish under any conceivable condition. My wife says he thinks like a fish and she might be right.

If thinking like a fish would make me a better fisherman, I'd be willing to give it a try. But, how does one learn to think like a fish? More to the point, how does a fish think?

Most research I've done on the subject indicates that fish act mostly from instinct. Their lives are guided by the phases of the moon, the tides, insect hatches and nature's other myriad phenomena. Scientists tell us fish can't reason . . . but I'm not sure.

My father and I spent two years trying to catch a big trout in the South Fork of the Payette River which Dad nicknamed "Old Toothless." The big fish out-foxed us at every turn. On one occasion the fish made such a monkey out of me that you never would have convinced my father the fish hadn't planned the action.

Dad had hooked Old Toothless in the big swimming hole at Gallagher Flats. The fish made a couple of powerful runs, dove under a sunken log, went back over the top and then under again. The fish ended up lying still finning gently in the slow current and, as Dad put it, laughing at us.

The fish was in about eight feet of water and we couldn't do a thing to land it . . . from the riverbank.

"Do you suppose you could untangle it?" Dad asked with a wide-eyed expression.

In a split second, the implication of his suggestion was clear. "You expect 'me' to do down there?" I asked.

"Only if you want to," he replied, with an almost childlike innocence.

Of course, I didn't want to. Not having recently won any gold medals for swimming, I didn't relish the idea of messing around with fishing line, a sunken log and Old Toothless.

But being young and a bit more on the reckless side, (this episode occurred about 25 years ago), I stripped to my shorts and taking a deep breath, and Dad's pocket knife, dove in and swam down to the log. My plan of action was to cut Dad's line and somehow haul the big trout back to shore.

When I cut the line, the fish made a quick turn, brushing past me on it's way to apparent freedom. As it went by I felt a sudden tug on my shorts and instantly realized my plan had not been flawless. I had forgotten to cut off Dad's second hook.

I had known from the beginning that it would be trickly to play the fish back to shore, but it never entered my mind that I'd be "playing both ends against the middle."

At this point, I lost interest in landing Dad's fish. Self preservation, being the powerful drive it is, motivated me to quickly shed my shorts. Drawers in hand I popped to the surface for some much needed air. With Old Toothless tugging on my drawers it was difficult to get my bearing.

"Did you get him?" my father yelled.

Now Dad could have said almost anything else and I wouldn't have reacted. When he asked me "if I had his fish?" . . . I cracked up. I laughed so hard I had to turn loose of my shorts to keep from drowning.

My father was red-faced and almost doubled up with laughter when he pulled me ashore.

The last thing we saw of Old Toothless was a final, spiteful leap at mid-pool. The fish took off downstream, my polka-dots creating a wake behind him.

My father passed away in 1964 and every now and then I have this wild dream. In it, Dad is fishing a beautiful, emerald-green river, catching big, wild trout on every cast. The only thing is . . . every rainbow he hooks is wearing red and white polka-dot shorts.

PART IV
ENTOMOLOGY AND
FLYTYING

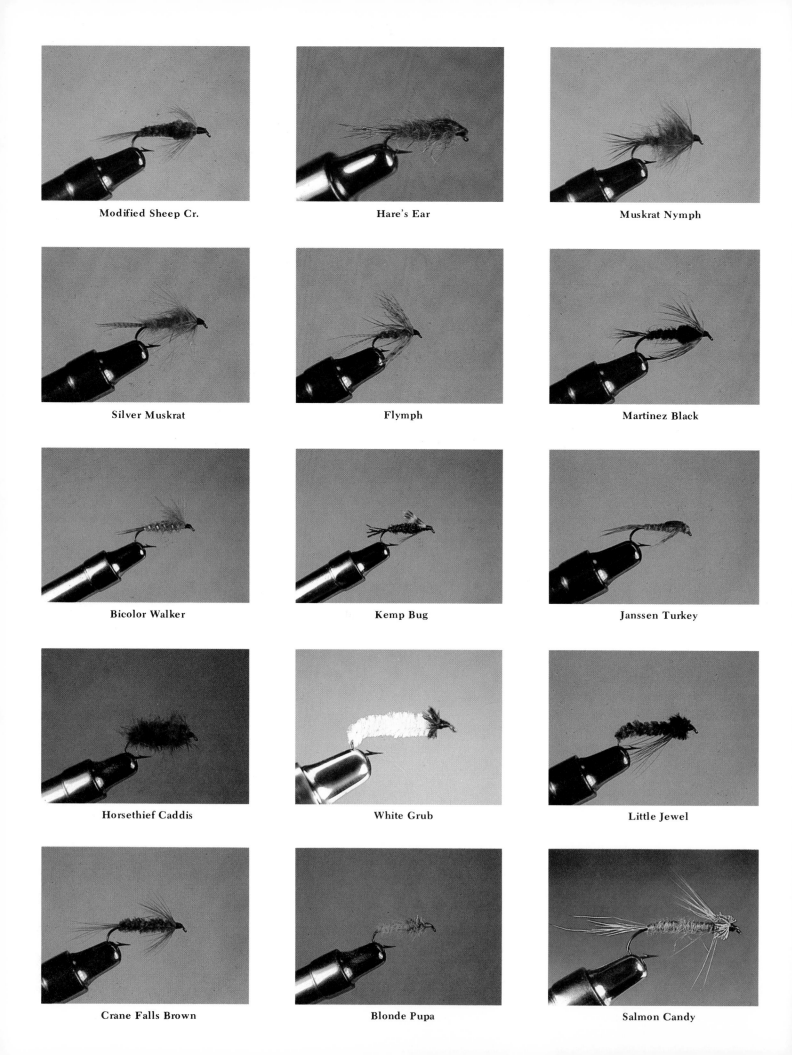

Modified Sheep Cr.

Hare's Ear

Muskrat Nymph

Silver Muskrat

Flymph

Martinez Black

Bicolor Walker

Kemp Bug

Janssen Turkey

Horsethief Caddis

White Grub

Little Jewel

Crane Falls Brown

Blonde Pupa

Salmon Candy

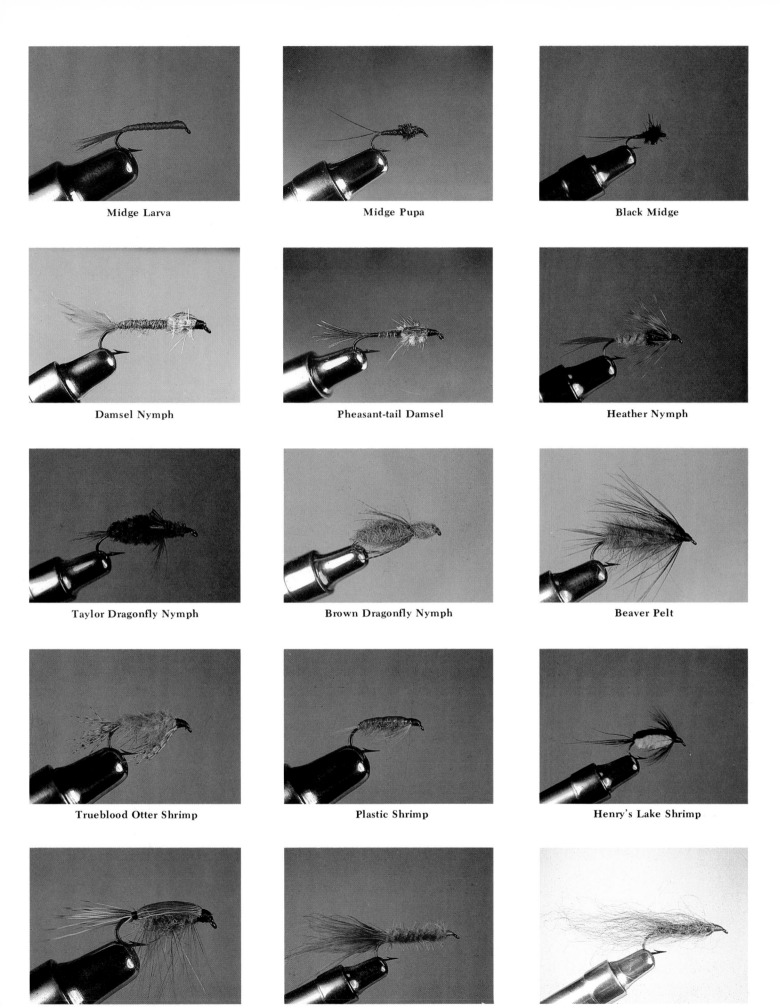

Midge Larva

Midge Pupa

Black Midge

Damsel Nymph

Pheasant-tail Damsel

Heather Nymph

Taylor Dragonfly Nymph

Brown Dragonfly Nymph

Beaver Pelt

Trueblood Otter Shrimp

Plastic Shrimp

Henry's Lake Shrimp

Werner Shrimp

Henry's Lake Leech

Canadian Brown Leech

Mohair Leech

Grouse Backswimmer

Zug Bug

Prince Nymph

Tellico

Pheasant-tail Crayfish

Taylor Snail

Stayner Ducktail

Spruce Fly

Integration

Malheur Streamer

Marabou Muddler

Tex's Favorite

Taylor Full Thorax Tex

Sheep Creek Special

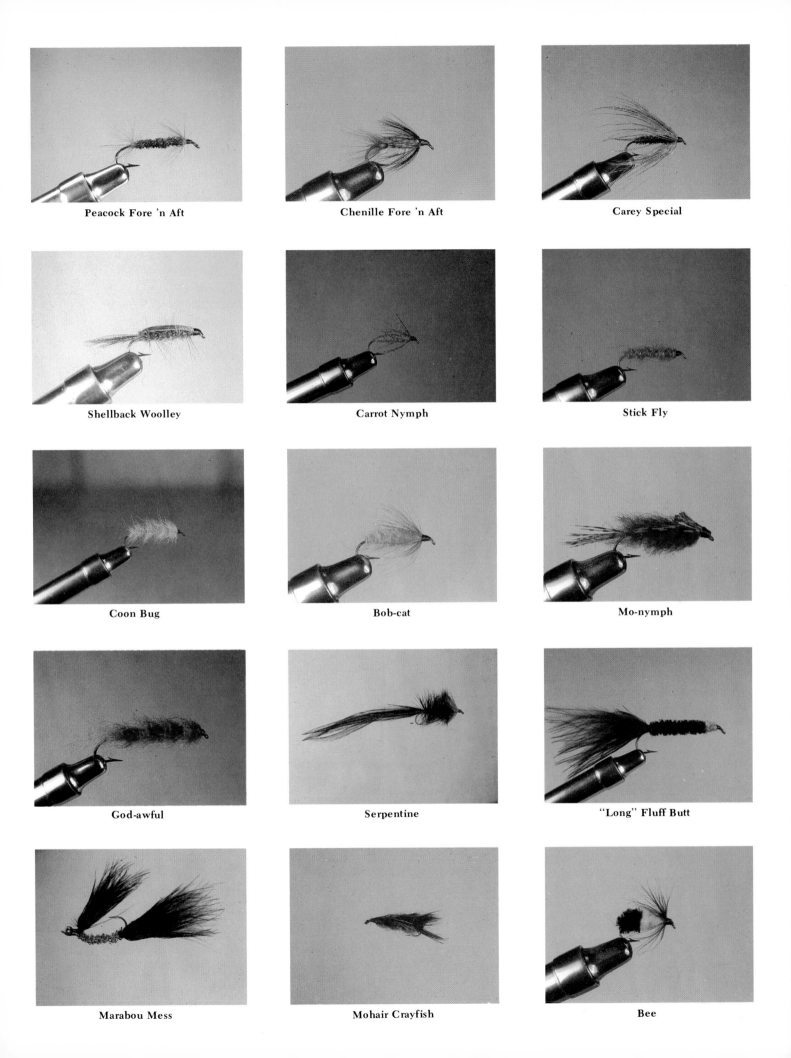

Peacock Fore 'n Aft

Chenille Fore 'n Aft

Carey Special

Shellback Woolley

Carrot Nymph

Stick Fly

Coon Bug

Bob-cat

Mo-nymph

God-awful

Serpentine

"Long" Fluff Butt

Marabou Mess

Mohair Crayfish

Bee

Chapter 22

Introduction to Entomology
and Flytying

Webster's defines entomology as "that branch of zoology which treats of insects and their habits." If you ask the average fisherman to define entomology, he likely will shrug it off as "something to do with bugs."

The ichthyologist knows it's a great deal more . . . as does Ernie Schweibert my favorite reference author. A basic knowledge of the subject is a vital weapon for the serious fly fisherman in his battles with the piscatorial adversary.

Most fly fishermen know the difference between an adult mayfly and an adult damselfly, but many are hard pressed to describe either in it's larval form. Few really know the difference between a fairy shrimp and a scud. Fewer still give a damn.

Therein lies the reason that 85 percent of the fishermen catch only 15 percent of the fish while the other 15 percent, who "do" give a damn, catch the remaining 85 percent.

I used to believe in "fishermen's luck," that so-called experts caught more fish because the "Man above" had taken a particular liking to them, or that they had a more pleasant odor on their hands that made bait an "offer fish couldn't refuse." Then I bought a copy of Ernie's book NYMPHS and discovered that a lot more goes on down under than I'd ever suspected. I began to wonder how I had ever managed to catch fish.

According to students of ichthyology, fish strike lures because of several basic drives including: hunger, greed, anger and curiosity. The fifth drive is habit . . . simple reflex action. The fish's brain says something has appeared in it's window of vision that is edible, and the fish strikes even if it isn't hungry. All five drives are important to fishermen.

When trout are ravenously hungry, it doesn't take an expert to catch them. At times like that an understanding of entomology and how it applies to fly fishing isn't necessary.

But when there is no hatch or other guide-line and most fishermen are having a tough time, talk to the one "lucky" guy who is catching fish, and I'll bet the proverbial "dollar to the hole in the doughnut" that he understands entomology

I've seen it happen dozens of times. One occasion that comes to mind was a day on Hosmer Lake in central Oregon. Hal Janssen, one of California's fine stillwater nymph fishermen, and I were fishing for Hosmer's famous land-locked Atlantic Salmon. On arriving at the lake, Hal studied the water for about fifteen minutes and then told me: "There's a false hatch of callibaetis mayflies going on."

I told him he was crazy, that I knew what a mayfly looked like, and that I sure didn't see any around.

Hal said I hadn't been listening. He emphasized it was a "false hatch."

I'd never heard of such a thing.

Hal explained that at times mayfly nymphs rise toward the surface as if to hatch, but at the last second, change their minds (or whatever insects reason with) and drop back to the bottom. Hal showed me a pattern he ties that imitates the callibaetis nymph in the posture of settling and offered to bet me he'd catch fish with it.

Since I knew Hal had an aquarium in his home filled with an assortment of nymphs in various stages, and since I had fished with him before, I knew better than to get suckered into such a bet.

Hal tied on the size 14 "turkey" nymph and proceeded to hook fish almost at will. Seven other boats were on Hosmer that day, and while my partner hooked and released over 30 salmon, (Hosmer is a barbless fly, catch and release fishery) all of the other fishermen, including me, caught only six. The lesson was deeply etched in my memory banks.

Nine basic food sources are important to stillwater fly fishermen. They are: mayflies; caddis flies; damselflies; dragonflies; midges; crustaceans, (freshwater shrimp, scuds etc.); leeches; backswimmers, (Hemipter family); and forage fish. Expert float-tube fishermen should be well acquainted with each group.

Sometimes the study of stillwater entomology can get so interesting that I forget other, more important, things. Several years ago I was fishing Henry's Lake during its famous "tan damsel hatch." The fishing was good, but I spent one entire afternoon watching damsel nymphs crawl ashore, hatch out and awkwardly fly away. When I got back to our camper, Vina asked me where our fish dinner was. I showed her the labor of my afternoon — three small specimen bottles full of damsel nymphs.

To this day, Vina says she doesn't understand fly fishermen.

When I first began tying flies, my patterns were simple — uncomplicated to the point they provoked icy stares from more knowledgeable tyers. I recall a reaction to one of my early and most productive flies. I was one of the few anglers catching fish one day, and my pattern was a variation of the Sheep Creek Special, listed under the "nondescripts." The tie, however, wasn't even close. I had the tail wrong and had substituted grizzly fibers for the regular mallard flank fiber wing.

But my fly was catching fish . . . lots of fish.

I had just released a two-pound rainbow when a voice caused me to turn.

"Hi Marv, how ya doin?"

I didn't immediately respond to the other tuber.

"Keith Whittaker . . . " he answered my blank stare.

Since Keith was one of the fly fishermen generally credited with developing the "Idaho float-tube system," I was a bit reluctant to show my fly to him. It was crude, and Keith was extremely proficient at combining bits and pieces of feathers and fur into successful flies.

"Well . . . it does look buggy," he said with a condescending tone. As he passed it back and began sorting through his fly boxes, he noticed my line. "You're using a 'fisherman'?" (a super slow sinker)

"I guess so . . ."

"It doesn't go very deep."

"I'm catching fish."

"So you are . . . let me see your fly again."

Since that day I've spent thousands of hours learning to tie flies, writing about them in my newspaper column and dressing them commercially. Most of what I've learned has come from other flytiers. I've picked brains and separated the wheat from the chaff — when I could tell one from the other.

I've borrowed the really good patterns, that fit into the Idaho system of float-tube fishing, redesigned some and "invented" a few. (Invention is a misnomer since all combinations of materials and basic patterns have been tied. Only the "Creator"

86

could design "new flies" since in essence it would take new "bugs". What the innovative tyer does is "improve" the basic patterns with new and better looking or longer lasting materials.)

My assortment of float-tube stillwater nymphs have been proven over the past decade in most of the lakes, ponds, and reservoirs within a 500-mile radius of my home in Boise.

Some of the patterns are "imitative" in design and some are merely "suggestive." Others are enigmatic patterns that fit under the heading "nondescript." While it is something of a mystery why some of these nondescripts appeal to fish, the good stillwater fisherman's fly boxes will contain many examples.

A beginning tyer should spend a good deal of time dressing the chenille-bodied patterns. By changing the color of the chenille and hackle, the tyer can "suggest" a wide assortment of nymphs — some of which are the best float-tube patterns.

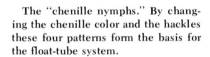
The "chenille nymphs." By changing the chenille color and the hackles these four patterns form the basis for the float-tube system.

After the novice has acquired some degree of talent in tying chenille flies, he can progress to more complicated patterns using dubbed fur and mohair.

To many non-tyers the art of dressing flies is somewhat mystical and often considered too difficult for all but the most dexterous. Nothing could be further from the truth. With proper tools anyone can become a good tyer. In demonstrations I often select a youngster, usually a 10 or 12 year old, and show them step by step how to tie a woolly worm. I then have the youngster sit down and tie one. The youths and onlookers usually are amazed at the positive results.

Fortunately for people desiring to tie flies, the initial cost for equipment and materials is relatively modest. This is not to say that some people who become enthusiastic about their hobby do not make a substantial investment in hooks, furs and feathers.

The most important and most expensive piece of equipment is a good flytiers vise. To be termed "good" a vise must be able to hold so firmly that the hook will bend or break before it will slip. The vise's jaws must be tapered in such a manner as to permit placing the thumb and forefinger along the shank of even the smallest hook. The jaws also must be long enough and deep enough to cover not only the point of the hook, but also the lower portion of the bend.

Next in importance to the vise are the hackle pliers, which hold feathers and other delicate bits of material during the tying operation. Hackle pliers can be tested by grasping a hair at different points in their jaws, to ensure a uniform, secure fit.

Other important tools include: a pair of high quality, straight bladed and sharply pointed scissors about 3½ inches long; a pair of flat tweezers; a dubbing needle; hook hone; used safety razor blade, and a bobbin.

The materials list for tying stillwater nymphs is much less complex — and less expensive — than for dressing dry flies.

Besides various colored chenilles in small, medium and large sizes, the beginner can get by with an assortment of furs including: muskrat; beaver; raccoon; otter; seal; opossum; badger; bobcat; dyed rabbit, and hare's mask.

He should buy the less expensive hen hackle necks and saddle hackle capes in the basic colors. He should have both mallard and woodduck flank feathers as well as the tail and rump of the ring-neck pheasant.

In his flytying kit he should also have: deer hair; squirrel tails; black bear hair; moose mane; guinea feathers; turkey quills; marabou; duck primarys; partridge hackle and an assortment of wool yarns.

To dress float-tube mohair nymphs the tyer should acquire an extensive collection of mohair yarns.

Finally, he should have good assortments of: floss; tinsel; buttonhole silk; peacock and ostrich herls; raffia; tying thread; wax and hooks.

Chapter 23

Mayflies

Although the "complete entomologist" should study every mayfly species, the "stillwater" callibaetis is most important to the tube fisherman. This little "speckled-wing" mayfly is found in nearly every lake and pond in the country, but western fly fishermen take it most seriously.

This genus is many brooded and takes only five to six weeks for a complete life cycle, which means that as many as three separate hatches can occur during a single season. My records show callibaetis hatches as early as May (in some of our lowland reservoirs) and as late as October.

The life cycle of the mayfly is unique. It has four stages: egg; nymph; subimago, (dun); and imago, (spinner). The life cycle begins with mid-air mating. Soon thereafter, the female, her body packed with a multitude of eggs, descends to the surface and deposits her eggs. The nymphs are hatched in a few weeks, and for the next year or so the nymphs molt as many as 15 or 20 times. During this growth process, they are lively underwater bugs and fall prey to fish and other carnivorous nymphs.

When the nymph finally develops wing pads and rises to the surface, it splits its outer skin from thorax to head and emerges as a subimago or dun. A few hours later it completes the final stage of life and is transformed into a beautiful imago or spinner. The final act of life is to join the great, swarming mating flight.

The float-tube fly fisherman utilizes the callibaetis in several ways. He can fish patterns such as the hare's ear or muskrat, both near the bottom and as an emerger. When fish are taking mature mayflies, the tuber should switch from sinking lines to floaters with dry flies. Some of my best days were due to heavy callibaetis hatches.

But another aspect of this little mayfly hatch has given me even better stillwater days. When the little callibaetis nymph begins its upward movement before hatching it turns on another of my favorite lake and pond insects — the dragonfly nymph. This large, carnivorous nymph sometimes feeds very actively, darting around devouring mayfly nymphs by the dozens.

I recognized this phenomenon for the first time while fishing Idaho's Horsethief Reservoir. A heavy callibaetis hatch was coming off, but neither I nor my companions were having any luck with normal mayfly patterns. For one reason or another, I tried one of my large, chenille dragonfly-nymph patterns. I fished it with a darting retrieve and couldn't keep the fish off. I was careful to remember the technique.

The best analogy (for this situation) would be offering a hard working truck driver the choice between a sixteen-ounce steak and a three-ounce hamburger. It doesn't take much imagination to predict which he will choose.

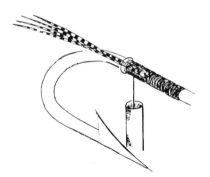

Modified Sheep Creek

Species:	Mayfly.

Data

Type:	Suggestive.
Line:	Fast sinking.
Retrieve:	The standard retrieve with 8-inch rips interspersed with the normal 3-inch.
Time:	Full season.

Description

Hook:	Sizes 8-12, 3X long.
Thread:	Black.
Tail:	10-15 light-olive hackle fibers.
Body:	Medium sized, dark-olive chenille, trimmed to a tapered shape.
Thorax:	Medium sized, dark-olive chenille, untrimmed.
Wing case:	Short tuft of wooduck dyed mallard flank feathers.
Hackle:	Medium-olive hackle fibers, tied beard style.
Head:	Black.

The Modified takes it's name from the Sheep Creek Special, listed later in the nondescript section. It is an excellent suggestive pattern for either mayfly nymphs or caddis pupas. When fishing these mayfly nymphs, the angler should remember to fish the fly all the way to the surface. Trout have a tendency to delay striking until the nymph is attempting to shed it's nymphal shuck.

To center tail fibers, place them slightly off center as you begin the wrap. The pressure of the thread, as it tightens, will "center" the fibers.

Hare's Ear

Species:	Mayfly

Data

Type:	Suggestive.
Line:	Floating or medium sinking.
Retrieve:	Hand twist or varied. Occasionally dead drift.
Time:	All season.

Description:

Hook:	Sizes 8-14, 2X long. Weighted or unweighted.
Thread:	Black or Brown.
Tail:	Clump of hare's mask.
Body:	Dubbing of medium grayish hare's ear, ribbed with gold oval tinsel or fine wire.
Thorax:	Dubbing of medium grayish hare's ear, slightly larger than body
Wing case:	Natural pheasant-tail fibers tied down at both ends.
Legs:	Longer guard hairs picked out of thorax
Head:	Black or brown.

The Hare's Ear probably is the most effective, most widely used all-purpose nymph the float-tuber can carry in his fly boxes. It encompasses all of the criteria for a successful nymph. It conforms to the shape of the mayfly, the natural color of the fur suggests a great many mayfly nymphs, and it is "buggy."

I dress half of my patterns weighted, identifying them by using a brown head instead of the normal black. Other variations include: a pheasant-tail fiber tail, silver ribbing, and pheasant-tail legs.

In dressing patterns with "full" dubbed bodies I use the loop method of preparing my dubbing.

In dubbing fur or hair, form a loop with tying thread and secure material by applying pressure with thumb. Twist loop to form "noodle."

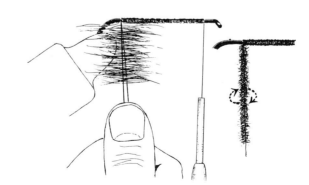

Muskrat No. 1

Species:	Mayfly.

Data

Type:	Suggestive.
Line:	Floating or slow sinking.
Retrieve:	Hand twist or varied. Occasionally dead drift.
Time:	From early spring until late fall.

Description

Hook:	Sizes 8-16, regular shank. Weighted or unweighted.
Thread:	Black or brown.
Tail:	Brown hackle fibers.
Body:	Dubbed muskrat fur, full.
Hackle:	Brown hackle, sparsely tied.
Head:	Black or brown.

The first muskrat nymph I ever dressed took a four-pound rainbow on my first cast. I've been a champion of the pattern ever since.

There are several variations of the pattern, and they all seem to catch fish. Variation No. 2 changes only the body. I twist the "noodle" tighter and end up with a tapered body, ribbed with fine gold wire or gray tying thread. Variation No. 3 substitutes grizzly hackle for both tail and hackle. It can be tied with either body style described above.

I fish number two as a deep nymph and number one as an emerger.

Float-tube fly fishing is a family affair. Darrell and Barbara Grim prepare for a day of bluegill fishing.

Silver Muskrat Emerger

    Species: Mayfly.

    Data
    Type: Suggestive.
    Line: Floating or slow sinking.
    Retrieve: Hand twist or varied. Occasionally dead drift.
    Time: From late spring until early fall.

    Description
    Hook: Sizes 8-16, 2X long.
    Thread: Black.
    Tail: Woodduck flank feather fibers or dyed mallard, 8 or 10.
    Body: Dubbed otter fur, medium thin body.
    Thorax: Dubbed muskrat fur, slightly larger than body.
    Hackle: Ginger hackle, sparsely tied.
    Head: Black.

    I've noticed the Silver Muskrat produces well on especially bright days. It may be that the old steelhead adage, "bright flies on bright days, dark flies on dark days," holds true with nymph patterns.

    I originally tied the body from a piece of silver muskrat given to me by a friend. When I ran out of the material I substituted otter and found it worked as well.

    I fish the fly primarily as an emerger, working it in or just below the surface film.

    In order to form a nicely tapered head, tie material off with three wraps, then bend it back placing three wraps in front. The technique works with chenille and dubbing as well as hackles.

Flymph

    Species: Mayfly. (Also an excellent pattern to suggest small caddis larva.)

    Data
    Type: Suggestive.
    Line: Floating or slow sinking.
    Retrieve: Hand twist or Leisenring Lift.
    Time: Late spring until early fall.

Description

Hook:	Sizes 12-16, regular shank.
Thread:	Appropriate color.
Tail:	Two or three soft hen hackle fibers, woodduck flank feather fibers, or mallard flank feather fibers, of appropriate color.
Body:	Dubbed fur of appropriate color. Ribbed with fine gold wire or button-hole silk.
Hackle:	Appropriate hen or cock hackle, sparsely dressed.
Head:	Appropriate color.

There are at least a dozen reasons for my being vague in tying description for this fly. Twelve is the number of Pete Hidy-tied flymphs hanging on my office wall. They include both the Hare's Ear and Blue Duns in light, medium and dark, the Tups Special, Pale Evening Dun, Light Ginger, Mahogony, Gray, and Iron Blue Dun.

Pete Hidy, a Boise resident, in collaboration with Jim Leisenring authored the fine little book THE ART OF TYING THE WET FLY AND FISHING THE FLYMPH. His patterns are dressed with fur bodies and soft hackles that trap air creating an illusion of nymphs struggling to the surface in a gaseous envelope of air.

I would suggest the reader who follows my recommendations on this pattern dress reasonable quantities. The last time I fished this fly, I went through a dozen and a half in less than two hours. The fish were super selective in their feeding and it took a 6X tippet to entice a strike . . . more often than not, the strike was all I ended up with.

Martinez Black Nymph

Species:	Mayfly.

Data

Type:	Suggestive.
Line:	Floating and medium sinking.
Retrieve:	Various.
Time:	A very good pattern for early season.

Description

Hook:	Sizes 8-12, 2X long.
Thread:	Black.
Tail:	Few wisps of black and white spotted guinea feather, medium short.
Body:	Dubbed black fur, ribbed with fine oval copper or gold tinsel.
Thorax:	Medium black chenille.
Hackle:	Light partridge hackle, sparsely tied.
Wing case:	Green raffia, over thorax, both ends tied down.
Head:	Black.

Originated by the famed West Yellowstone guide and flytier, Don Martinez. Don originally dressed the body with dyed-black seal fur. I use this pattern extensively in the spring on lowland lakes and reservoirs in my area when the occasion calls for a black nymph.

94

Bicolor Walker

Species: Mayfly.

Data
Type: Suggestive.
Line: Floating.
Retrieve: Hand twist or dead drift.
Time: Late June through July.

Description
Hook: Sizes 8-10, 3X long.
Thread: Black.
Tail: Short brown-dyed cock pheasant breast fibers.
Body: Brownish wine-colored fuzzy yarn. Ribbed with corn yellow buttonhole twist silk thread.
Wing case: Tuft of purplish-brown fluff from butt of hackle.
Head: Black.

Originated by E. H. (Polly) Rosborough of Chiloquin, Oregon, who says the nymph seems to be restricted to a definite latitude. It occurs nationwide from Oregon to New York, but not south of these states. The pattern should be dressed smaller in the east. The nymph begins to emerge soon after sundown, and the mating hatch occurs at night. The insect changes little in color or appearance from nymph to spinner. The adults are large with upright soot-colored wings. This fly should be fished in the top one-inch of water from late June through July.

Janssen Turkey Callibaetis

Species: Mayfly.

Data
Type: Imitative.
Line: Medium sinking.
Retrieve: Hand twist or standard.
Time: All season.

Description
Hook: Sizes 12-16, 2X long. Weighted.
Thread: Tan.
Tail: Turkey fibers.
Body: Turkey fibers, wound on, tapered slightly.
Thorax: Turkey fibers, slightly larger than body.
Wing case: Gray goose quill section.
Legs: Partridge hackle fibers.

Originated by Hal Janssen, one of my good friends from northern California, the Turkey Callibaetis is an excellent imitator of several of the western speckled wing mayflies.

The pattern should be weighted with .016-inch fuse wire which doubles as an underbody for the thorax.

An alternate variation has the legs folded back and is the "hatching" pattern. The drawing demonstrates the "false hatching" mayfly described at the beginning of this chapter.

Kemp Bug

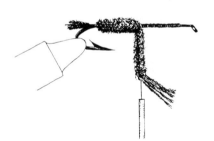

Species: Mayfly.

Data
Type: Suggestive.
Line: Floating and deep sinking.
Retrieve: Various.
Time: All season, particularly during spring and early summer.

Description
Hook: Sizes 8-12, 2X long.
Thread: Black.
Tail: Three short peacock herl spikes.
Body: Peacock herl tapered full at thorax.
Wing Case: Short grizzly hackle tips, tied flat.
Hackle: Furnace, beard style, tied sparse.
Head: Black.

Another of the dark mayfly nymph patterns that produce especially well during spring. The "big three" of the early season peacock bodied nymphs include the Zug Bug, the Prince Nymph and the Kemp Bug.

To dress a more permanent peacock body, twist herls around tying thread and wrap as with any other body material.

96

Chapter 24

Caddis Flies

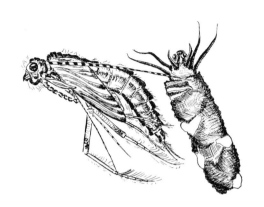

For many years most of the emphasis in tying flies was on the mayfly. The caddis fly probably was ignored because the hatches are less dramatic than mayfly hatches and because when both are hatching, trout may take a mayfly imitation for either insect.

Early fly tyers may have thought they didn't need to dress an adult caddis. They may have been right regarding the mature insect, but this cannot be said of the larval or pupal stages. When trout are feeding on Rhyacophila larvae, for example, you had better have a bright green caddis worm on the end of your line if you are interested in catching fish.

Although the caddis have no real "nymph" stage, the insect undergoes complete metamorphosis from egg to larvae to pupa to adult. The larva is taken by trout while wrapped in its case, and the pupa is engorged just before the hatch. As in the mayfly cycle, the caddis pupae have a vulnerable period when they drift along before splitting their shucks.

The presence of caddis in a lake is easily established. They are the case builders, whose portable "houses" of sand, pebbles, twigs and vegetation are found along the bottom or clinging to vegetation. The larvae cement their dwellings in place when they are ready to mature, but trout eat them, houses and all.

In the early part of the trout season when tubing lowland reservoirs, I begin with a dark olive-green woolly worm in size 10 or 12. If fish are feeding on cased caddis larva, a fast-sinking line will take the fly right to them. Other colors used to imitate the cased caddis are: dark or medium brown, gray and black.

The transformation from larva to pupa is not unlike the transformation from caterpillar to chrysalis among moths and butterflies. Pupal forms vary considerably from the larva and they stop eating and enter a brief, hibernation-like cycle. Pupation can take from a few weeks to the entire winter.

The morphologial structure of the pupa bears a considerable resemblance to the adult form. The thorax and abdomen are distinctly formed, evolving wings are readily visible inside the pupal skin, and both the antennae and the legs lie parallel to the body, trailing past the posterior abdominal segment. The legs are heavily fringed at this stage, which permits the pupa to swim easily toward the surface.

Such pupae emerge in two ways. Some species emerge in open water, using the tension of the surface film to split their pupal skins. Others creep out of the water to plant stems, rocks or deadfalls to hatch.

Float-tube fishermen should dress their patterns to duplicate both the cased larva and the emerging pupa. The patterns include: the Salmon Candy; Blonde Pupa; Little Jewel; White Grub; Horsethief Caddis, and Crane Falls Brown.

Salmon Candy — Stage No. 1

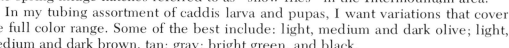

Species: Caddis Fly.

Data
Type: Suggestive.
Line: Floating and slow sinking.
Retrieve: Hand twist and standard.
Time: All season.

Description
Hook: Sizes 8-10, 3X long.
Thread: Black.
Tail: Deer body hairs, short and sparse.
Body: Medium size, dark-olive wool.
Hackle: One turn of brown hackle.
Thorax: Form sparse collar of deer hair, similar to the
      Muddler Minnow.
Head: Black.

First dressed by Lloyd Frese, Bend, Oregon, this fly is dressed to represent various stages of the caddis fly.

Stage No. 2 description: tail same; body, same; hackle, brown palmered, sparse; overbody, deer body hair, pulled over underbody, tied off at head, leaving small, clipped head.

Blonde Pupa

Species: Caddis Fly.

Data
Type: Suggestive.
Line: Floating and slow sinking.
Retrieve: Hand twist and standard.
Time: All season.

Description
Hook: Sizes 10-14, 1X long.
Thread: Tan.
Body: Soft cream underbody of bobcat, dubbed and tapered
      larger toward thorax. May be ribbed with tan
      tying thread.
Hackle: Light cahill hackle, 2 wraps, trimmed top and bottom.
Thorax: Light cahill hackle, bunched tight, trimmed similar
      to the head on a Muddler Minnow.
Head: Tan.

This is good early season caddis pupa suggestor. Most large reservoirs in the Northwest have good early season caddis hatches. The pattern also is useful to imitate spring midge hatches referred to as "snow flies" in the Intermountain area.

In my tubing assortment of caddis larva and pupas, I want variations that cover the full color range. Some of the best include: light, medium and dark olive; light, medium and dark brown, tan; gray; bright green, and black.

The emphasis on my stillwater nymph selection of float-tube flies is simplicity. What I try to do with my pattern system is weed out the flies I don't need, rather than tie new ones. One day I hope to pare my assortment down to a "top two dozen."

"Changing flies" doesn't catch fish . . . "fishing them" does.

Horsethief Cased Caddis

Species:	Caddis Fly.

Data

Type:	Suggestive.
Line:	Medium fast sinking.
Retrieve:	Hand twist or dead drift.
Time:	Late spring through midsummer.

Description

Hook:	Sizes 8-12, 1X long. Weighted or unweighted.
Thread:	Black or brown.
Body:	Underbody of medium-olive marabou. Dark-olive chenille is wound over the marabou with some fibers sticking out.
Hackle:	Dark-olive dyed hackle, palmered and clipped short.
Head:	Black or brown.

A very good early season producer when trout are feeding heavily on cased caddis'.

Some excellent variations include shades of brown and gray.

The technique for tying the Horsethief Cased Caddis is useful in dressing other woolly worm types. A bit of marabou showing through the palmered hackle can "improve" almost any woolly worm pattern.

White Grub

Species:	Caddis Fly.

Data

Type:	Imitative.
Line:	Floating or slow sinking.
Retrieve:	Hand twist or dead drift.
Time:	All season.

Description

Hook:	Sizes 8-14, 1X long.
Thread:	Black.
Body:	White chenille or wool yarn, ribbed with silver wire.
Hackle:	Black hackle feather, 3 wraps, clipped short.
Head:	Black.

This pattern imitates the white larva of the caddis fly. It should be fished slowly and with great deliberation. I've had better luck with this fly during late afternoon and early evening.

Little Jewel

Species:	Caddis Fly.

Data

Type:	Suggestive.
Line:	Fast sinking.
Retrieve:	Hand twist or varied.
Time:	All season.

Description

Hook:	Sizes 8-12, 2X long. Weighted or unweighted.
Thread:	Black or brown.
Body:	Dark olive-green chenille, ribbed with gold oval tinsel or dark olive-green floss or buttonhole twist silk thread.
Hackle:	Brown hackle feather, 3 wraps trimmed on top and bottom.
Thorax:	Medium or large black chenille.
Head:	Black or brown.

As with the other chenille bodied patterns this one has many variations. It can be dressed with bodies of brown, gray, tan, black, bright green, light olive-green or varigated chenilles. It can be dressed with the conventional black thorax or one that matches the body. The hackle also can be varied to match the body.

I first dressed this pattern in spring 1971 and later named it the Little Jewel in honor of Jewel Lake in Northern Idaho. Ken Magee and I had been taking fish with the pattern regularly and thought it deserved a name. We happened to be fishing Jewel Lake when the urge to name the fly became more than we could resist.

**Alternate dressing of Little Jewel is
of matching chenilles and hackle.**

make no mistake about their importance to trout. They are available all season long and are a major ingredient for fish's growth.

Flytiers can imitate a wide variety of midge larva with this one pattern. Everything from the Crane Fly Larva (Tipula bicornis) in size 10, to the Sand Gnat Larva (Culicoides minutes) in size 24.

Midge Pupa

Species	Midge (Diptera)

Data
Type:	Suggestive.
Line:	Floating and slow sinking.
Retrieve:	Hand twist and standard.
Time:	All season.

Description
Hook:	Sizes 12-20, 3X long.
Thread:	Black.
Tail:	Two moose mane fibers.
Body:	Appropriate color floss, thread or various materials, tapered slightly larger at thorax.
Thorax:	Peacock herls slightly larger than body.
Head:	Black.

I dress this pattern with body variations that include: black, brown, olive, tan, bright green and black. I also add two appropriately dyed grizzly hackle tips over the thorax, to some patterns. This would be the emerger phase of the nymph.

Black Midge

Species:	Midge (Diptera)

Data
Type:	Imitative.
Line:	Floating.
Retrieve:	Hand twist or dead drift.
Time:	All season.

Description
Hook:	Sizes 16-20, 1X short.
Thread:	Black.
Tail:	3-4 black hackle fibers.
Body:	Moose mane or dark brown thread.
Thorax:	Black hackle wound thickly, clipped to size.
Hackle:	A few black hackles each side, not clipped.
Head:	Black.

Originated about 1958 by Gary Howells, Richmond, California, and Dan Bailey, Livingston, Montana, to duplicate the snow fly so important to winter fishermen. I also use this little midge for much of my summer high lake fishing. I find it effective as an "in-the-film" nymph or dressed to float.

Midge larva and pupa imitators are particularly effective on high lakes. Fishing them in the film often will take trout rising to dries when they refuse your best floating patterns.

Chapter 26

Dragonflies

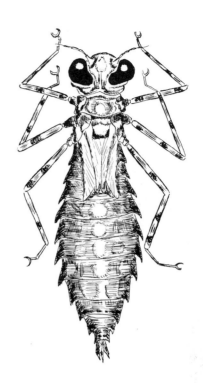

If a fisherman could see what's happening near the bottom of his favorite lake or
reservoir, he might be reminded of a science fiction movie.

The battle for survival among the many insects is unceasing. Hordes of tiny
midges and microcaddis make easy prey for carnivorous backswimmers, freshwater
shrimps and damsel nymphs. But the real killer of the depths is the dragonfly
nymph. A real terror, the Big D is a true gourmand. It feeds on nymphs of other
species, smaller specimens of it's own species and small fish fry.

Many fish culturists are convinced that nymphs of the Anisoptera (the dragonfly
species) are responsible for enormous losses in hatchery and stream-bred trout. Fly
fishermen who understand stillwater entomology, also account for fish losses by
using dragonfly-nymph imitations.

My first real exposure to dragonfly nymphs in lake fishing was at North Silver
Lake near Spokane, Washington. I spent several days fishing with Bill Butler, the
owner of the boat dock on the lake.

One morning Bill asked me to help him accumulate his daily supply of live bait.
We took a boat out to a section of lily pads and began gently pulling up weeds from
which we gathered several hundred fat, olive-green nymphs about two-inches in
length. "Probably the best live bait outside of minnows," Bill said. "You'll do well
to develop a pattern for your area." Subsequently I followed Bill's advice, and the
results are described in the fly-pattern section of this chapter.

Adult dragonflies are considerably larger than damselflies and highly predacious.
They dart back and forth snaring their prey in mid-air.

The nymphs have a unique swimming system. The lower intestine is thin-walled
and functions as a gill, absorbing oxygen from water taken in and expelled through
the anal orifice. The nymphs are stout and thick-set when compared with nymphal
forms of damselflies.

Most dragonflies are sluggish on the bottom, and imitations normally should be
fished slow and deep. But by utilizing their "jet-propulsion" system dragonfly
nymphs are capable of rapid, staccato swimming. At times, a fly fisherman should
fish dragonfly imitations in middle depths, with a retrieve suggestive of their agile
and erratic swimming.

My dragonfly nymph patterns, the Taylor Dragonfly nymph and Brown Dragonfly nymph, are both "imitative" and "suggestive" in design. My main concern is attempting to "imitate" a natural, is to emphasize its dominant characteristic. In the case of the Dragonfly nymph, a "fat" abdomen.

Other effective patterns include the beaverpelt and various mohair nondescripts.

Taylor Dragonfly Nymph

Species:	Dragonfly (Either Anax Junius or Aeschna Constricta)

Data
Type:	Imitative.
Line:	Deep sinking.
Retrieve:	Standard, varied and, at times, super-quick.
Time:	All season.

Description
Hook:	Sizes 6-12, 4X long. Weighted or unweighted.
Thread:	Black or brown.
Tail:	3-4 pheasant-tail fibers tied short. Natural or dark olive-green.
Body:	Underbody: wool yarn, tied football shape. Overbody: large size, dark olive-green chenille, trimmed flat on bottom.
Thorax:	Small size dark olive-green chenille.
Wing case:	Bunch of pheasant-tail fibers tied between body and thorax. Natural or dark olive-green.
Hackle:	Dark olive-green dyed grizzly hackle, 3 wraps, between body and thorax, clipped top and bottom. Brown hackle may be subbed.
Head:	Black or brown.

One of the theories practiced by many of the best float-tube fly rodders is "big fish want a mouthful, so fish a big fly." This particular dragonfly nymph pattern has "saved" the day for me on many occasions.

I fish it slowly along the bottom near weed beds and retrieve it with several variations. At times I find it most effective with the super quick retrieve.

There is one pattern variation I use that includes the addition of monofilament eyes. I form the eyes in the following manner:

Using short lengths of extra-heavy monofilament, paint ends with an appropriate color felt tip pen and hold over a candle until eyeball is formed.

Brown Dragonfly Nymph

Species: Dragonfly (Gomphus stygiatus)

Data
Type: Suggestive.
Line: Hi-density.
Retrieve: Hand twist or slow troll.
Time: All season.

Description
Hook: Sizes 8-10 3X long. Weighted or unweighted.
Thread: Black or brown.
Body: Dubbed brownish-olive mohair, football shaped.
Thorax: Dubbed brownish-olive mohair.
Hackle: Brown partridge, sparsely tied, trimmed on top
                and bottom.
Head: Black or brown.

This pattern imitates, or suggests, the Gomphus stygiatus dragonfly nymph, or any of the bottom crawlers of the species that are brown-toned. It should be fished with a deep sinking line right down on the bottom. The natural has an inclination to crawl down into the debris and silt and is sometimes hard to see even when you're looking right at it.

Beaverpelt

Species: Dragonfly.

Data
Type: Nondescript.
Line: Deep sinking.
Retrieve: Standard and varied.
Time: All season.

Description
Hook: Sizes 2-8, 2X long. Weighted or unweighted.
Thread: Black or brown.
Tail: Very short pheasant rump fibers.
Body: Dubbed dark beaver fur, thicker towards the head.
Hackle: Black hen hackle or pheasant rump feathers,
                sparsely tied.
Head: Black or brown.

Although this pattern usually is listed with the nondescripts, I think it is most important when trout are taking brown dragonfly nymphs. Created by Don E. Earnest, a fisheries biologist with the Washington State Department of Game it is a deadly "search" pattern.

I use four patterns when searching for feeding fish. I begin with a Tex's Favorite and follow up with a dragonfly nymph, a brown leech (a Henry's Lake Leech or a Canadian Brown) and a Stayner Ducktail. When I don't stir something up with this group of flies . . . not much is happening.

Chapter 27

Damselflies

The damselfly may not be the most important stillwater forms for the fly fisherman, but it certainly is the most fun to fish. When an armada of damsel nymphs invade a shoreline with big trout picking them off near the surface, the hackles on the neck of a float-tube fisherman may bristle in anticipation.

Pick a rising trout, cast ahead of it — you can usually determine the direction a fish is feeding after a couple of rises — work your nymph imitator with very short twitches and . . . stand ready for a shoulder-busting strike.

Damselflies are included in the Odonata order in the Zygoptera subfamily. The adults are the swift-winged "darning-needles" we all remember from our childhood. Most fishermen can recall the surface of their favorite trout or bluegill pond literally covered with blue, green and tan damselflies scurrying about in a "mating game."

The nymphs are agile swimmers, using their "rear-end" gills as sculling oars. Since the damselfly is predatory, it is active during every season of the year. I can remember doing an autopsy on a rainbow trout during December that was stuffed to the gills with damsel nymphs of all sizes. Since the insect is many-brooded, emergence occurs in several periods between April and November.

Damselfly nymphs vary in color from region to region and lake to lake. In the book *Nymphs*, Schweibert lists ten species ranging from purplish-black to pale yellow. In between are the bright olives, bright greens, ambers, light browns and dark browns.

My fly boxes includes a dozen color variations of the Taylor damsel nymph and the Pheasant-tail damsel in sizes 8 to 12.

Damsel Nymph

Species:	Damselfly.
Data	
Type:	Imitative.
Line:	Floating or slow sinking during the hatch. Deep sinking at other times.
Retrieve:	Hand twist or standard.
Time:	All season. Although the major hatch occurs during late June or July, some emergence may last until late September.

Description

Hook:	Sizes 8-12, 4X long.
Thread:	Black or color to match body.
Tail:	Light-olive marabou fibers.
Body:	Medium-olive wool yarn, thin body.
Thorax:	Light-olive chenille, large size.
Wing case:	Turkey or pheasant-tail fibers, tied down at both ends.
Hackle:	Light or medium-olive hackle palmered over thorax. It should be clipped to within 1¼-inch on sides and flattened on the bottom.
Head:	Black or color to match body.

The damsel hatch is, in my opinion, the most exciting part of the float-tuber's season. Watching big trout taking swimming damsel nymphs in shallow-water reed beds makes any trip. Hooking them is the frosting on the cake.

I've been questioned on two points of the dressing. First, why I trim my hackles when most other tiers leave them long? If you watch a damsel nymph swimming you will see it looks much like a tiny brownish-green pollywog with it's legs tucked back along it's sides. The trimmed hackle provides this allusion.

Secondly, I've been asked why I use light-olive chenille for the thorax when most other patterns maintain body color throughout the fly? I dress this pattern in several shades of brown as well as the olives. Most of the damsel nymphs I've collected are several shades lighter on their undersides and I feel my pattern more accurately imitates this coloration.

The damsel nymph swims with a "pollywog" action, using it's gills as sculling oars.

Pheasant-tail Damsel

Species:	Damselfly.

Data

Type:	Suggestive.
Line:	Floating or slow sinking during the hatch. Deep sinking at other times.
Retrieve:	Hand twist or standard.
Time:	All season. Major hatch during late June or July.

Description

Hook:	Sizes 8-16, 4X long.
Thread:	Black or brown.
Tail:	4-5 pheasant-tail fibers.
Body:	Pheasant-tail fibers wound on, tapering slightly larger at the thorax.
Thorax:	Light-olive chenille, large size.
Wing case:	Pheasant-tail fibers, tied down at both ends.
Hackle:	Brown hackle palmered over thorax. It should be clipped to within ¼-inch on sides and flattened on the bottom.
Head:	Black or brown.

In sizes 8 through 12, I use this pattern as a brown damsel nymph imitator. In sizes 14 and 16 I use it as an all-purpose pattern suggesting various mayfly nymphs.

Some controversy exists about weighting damselfly nymphs. Some experts indicate the natural nymph "dips" and "darts" when pursued, and therefore should be weighted at the thorax. My theory is that since the pattern is most useful in shallow water during the hatch, it should be dressed to hold it's position just under the surface.

On the other hand . . . it doesn't hurt to have some weighted versions for deep fishing — when the hatches end.

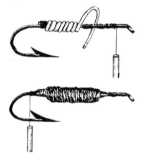

In weighting patterns fuse wire is wrapped tightly towards eye of hook, tied off and over-wrapped with thread to tail.

Heather Nymph

Species:	Damselfly.

Data

Type:	Suggestive.
Line:	Floating or deep sinking.
Retrieve:	Hand twist or varied retrieve.
Time:	All season in deeper water with success in shallow water during June and July hatches.

Description

Hook:	Sizes 8-12, 3X long.
Thread:	Black.
Tail:	Scarlet hackle fibers.
Body:	Insect green (chartreuse) spun fur, ribbed with fine oval tinsel.
Thorax:	Peacock herl.
Hackle:	Short grizzly hackle, 3 wraps.
Head:	Black.

Three float-tubers enjoying a sunny spring day on a southern Idaho Bass and bluegill pond.

Originated by Fenton Roskelley, Spokane, Washington, in 1960 it simulates the damsel nymph and other underwater forms. Variations include: rear half of the body, red or black spun fur.

Chapter 28

Crustaceans

rout gourmets look for two characteristics in their "eating fish." The fish must be firm and heavy, and must have a rich salmon-colored flesh.

Idaho's Henry's Lake and Silver Creek are examples of waters that produce such fish. They also have another thing in commom: they are rich in freshwater crustaceans.

Freshwater shrimp, scuds, sowbugs and crayfish are widely distributed in American waters, particularly those with high alkalinity and good oxygenation. I recall fishing Idaho's Richfield Canal, in the southern part of the state, and watching bait fishermen gather shrimp. Using long handled rakes and pitch-forks, they removed the moss, which teem with shrimp. They filled can after can with the tiny crustaceans and baited their hooks with ten or twelve of the little shrimp. They then would float them through the holes to willing trout. The fish they caught were deep-bodied and full of fight. They also are among the best eating trout in all of Idaho.

Crustaceans superficially resemble insects in their jointed appendages. They have broadly jointed heads but no neck structure. They breathe with a system of abdominal gills. Their bodies are encased in a hard exoskeleton secreted by a layer of cells just under its surface.

Crustaceans are divided into two main groups: larger types are classified under the malacostraca; the smaller forms are the entomostraca. Fly fishermen are primarily concerned with the former group, which includes crayfish, freshwater shrimp, scuds and sowbugs.

Since all these crustaceans swim backwards, their imitations should be tied accordingly. Dozens of excellent patterns with some new and interesting techniques are being tied, but I usually fall back on Ted Trueblood's Otter Shrimp as my favorite pattern.

In fishing shrimp or scuds, the best places to find fish, particularly larger trout in lakes and reservoirs, are near inlets and outlets. Crustaceans will be found in shallow water because photosyntheses depends on the penetration of sunlight into the aquatic ecosystem, and because insects and crustaceans and tiny fish find both food and shelter in the shallows.

The countdown method of fishing a freshwater shrimp or scud imitations, such as at Henry's Lake, is a matter of discipline and patience. Using a hi-density line the angler casts as far as his ability allows, makes his count-down — depending on the known depth of the lake — and retrieves with a jerky motion. (See chapter on retrieves.) He will add seconds if he doesn't hit bottom, subtract seconds if he does.

112

Trueblood Otter Shrimp

Species:	Freshwater shrimp and scud.

Data

Type:	Suggestive.
Line:	Hi-density.
Retrieve:	All variations, particularly the Henry's Lake rip.
Time:	All season.

Description

Hook:	Sizes 10-18, regular shank. Weighted or unweighted.
Thread:	Brown.
Tail:	Brown partridge feather fibers.
Body:	A mixture of otter and cream seal, loosely dubbed.
Hackle:	Brown partridge feather fibers tied beard style, three-fourths of way to hook point.
Head:	Dark olive or brown.

Since I've been dressing flies commercially I've tried dozens of shrimp and scud patterns and most have been successful at one time or another. When the fishing gets tough though, and I'm certain trout are taking a shrimp or scuds, I fall back to the otter.

Plastic Shrimp

Species:	Freshwater shrimp and scuds.

Data

Type:	Imitation.
Line:	Hi-Density.
Retrieve:	All variations, particularly the Henry's Lake rip.
Time:	All season.

Description

Hook:	Sizes 10-18, regular shank. Weighted or unweighted.
Thread:	Medium-olive.
Tail:	Light-olive hackle fibers.
Body:	Dubbed olive-brown fur, medium body. Shellback: clear plastic strip overlay. Ribbed with fine gold wire.
Beard:	Light-olive hackle fibers.
Head:	Medium-olive.

An excellent shrimp pattern for high mountain lakes. I've used it extensively in northern Idaho and eastern Washington. Excellent variations can be achieved by using darker hackles, darker fur, and darker plastic overlay. I mark my weighted patterns with a single wrap of red thread at the base of the head.

Skunk Shrimp

Species:	Freshwater shrimp and scuds.

Data

Type:	Suggestive.
Line:	Hi-density.
Retrieve:	Varied and Henry's Lake rip.
Time:	All season.

Description

Hook:	Sizes 8-12, regular shank. Weighted.
Thread:	Black.
Tail:	Black hackle fibers or black bear hair.
Body:	Fluorescent green chenille. Shellback of black bear hair or fine chenille.
Hackle:	One wrap black hackle.
Head:	Black.

Although this pattern was originated for Henry's Lake, I've taken trout with it in more than a dozen other lakes and reservoirs. An effective variation substitutes light-olive hackle for rib and tail.

The original Henry's Lake patterns had bodies of yellow, hot orange, red, insect green, brown, olive, or black. The shellback was gray squirrel or black hair divided at the head to form feelers. In my opinion the newer fluorescent bodies are far superior to the original tie.

Werner Shrimp

Species:	Freshwater shrimp and scuds.

Data

Type:	Suggestive.
Line:	Hi-density.
Retrieve:	Varied or Henry's Lake rip.
Time:	All season.

Description

Hook:	Sizes 10-12, regular shank. Weighted or unweighted.
Thread:	Black or brown.
Tail:	Deer body hair.
Body:	Olive seal fur, palmered sparsely with brown hackle. Shellback of deer body hair.
Head:	Black or brown.

Originated by Mary Stewart of Vancouver, B.C., it was popularized by Werner Schmid of Vancouver. The pattern is excellent in waters frequented by the Gray Freshwater Scud (gammarus fasciatus), one of the largest and most common of the crustaceans found in American waters.

Pheasant-tail Crayfish

Species: Crayfish.

Data
Type: Suggestive.
Line: Hi-density.
Retrieve: Standard and varied.
Time: All season.

Description
Hook: Sizes 8-12, 1X long. Weighted.
Thread: Black.
Tail: Pheasant-tail fibers, trimmed short and square
                     over the eye of the hook. (remember, the crayfish
                     swims backwards)
Body: Dark olive-green chenille.
Thorax: Dark olive-green chenille, larger than body.
Hackle: Furnace hackle, several turns over thorax.
Shellback: Pheasant-tail fibers length of body and thorax.
Pincers: Pheasant-tail fiber, tied as "V" at the bend of the hook.

An excellent pattern for both spiney rays and trout. It should be fished as close to the bottom as possible with a jerky motion interspersed with long pulls. It seems to take larger fish than many other stillwater patterns.

Chapter 29

Leeches

Although the leech isn't an insect, and technically doesn't belong in a section on entomology, it is a very important food item for stillwater trout and most other fish.

Leeches may be the least understood item on the trout's menu. Unless you are unfortunate enough to have one of the little bloodsuckers become "attached" to you, they are seldom noticed. Until I had such an encounter with a dozen of the little beasties in one of Idaho's mountain lakes, I assumed leeches were found only in old Humphrey Bogart movies.

Belonging to the phylum Annelida, leeches are an invertebrate, worm-like animal found in most lakes and ponds. They come in a wide variety of colors ranging from gray to brown to almost black. They are imitated on hooks ranging in size from 4 through 12, usually 3X or 4X long. I dress my patterns on as small a hook as possible and use a long bushy marabou tail. The marabou gives the fly an undulating motion similar to the swimming style of the natural.

In fishing the leech, work it from the bottom all the way to the surface. The most effective retrieves are the "hand-twist" and "standard."

When I'm "searching" for fish the leech pattern is one of the first flies I try.

Henry's Lake Leech

Species:	Leech.

Data

Type:	Imitative.
Line:	Hi-density.
Retrieve:	Hand twist or standard.
Time:	All season.

Description

Hook:	Sizes 6-12, 4X long. Weighted or unweighted.
Thread:	Brown.
Tail:	Rust-brown marabou.
Body:	Medium sized rust-brown chenille, palmered with clipped brown hackle.
Head:	Brown.

I learned to tie the "Jim Wright" version of "Big Red" at Henry's Lake in 1973. Although several color variations are used for this pattern, I have found Jim's tie to be the most effective. The dressing, as Jim showed it to me one August evening, is exactly as I describe above except that Jim uses a wool body.

The color variations I have in my fly boxes include: tan, standard brown, coachman brown, and black.

Although the Henry's Lake Leech carries the name of a specific body of water, it is useful anywhere leeches are found. As with most all of the flies in this book it has been proven by thousands of hours of fishing on every type of lake and pond.

Another excellent leech pattern was designed by Gary Howells, Richmond, California. The body is of rust brown rabbit dubbed into a medium-thin shape. One marabou "stem" is placed on the top and tied off at half a dozen places along the body. It takes a little longer to dress than the Henry's Lake Leech but is very effective.

Canadian Brown Leech

Species:	Leech.

Data

Type:	Suggestive.
Line:	Hi-density.
Retrieve:	Hand twist or standard.
Time:	All season.

Description

Hook:	Sizes 6-12, 4X long. Weighted or unweighted.
Thread:	Black or red.
Body:	Varigated mohair yarn, tied "stick-fly style" and picked out.
Head:	Black or red. (Red on weighted versions)

This pattern takes its name from the source of the mohair yarn used in the original dressing; an English yarn no longer in manufacture. For the past ten years local tyers have been obtaining skeins of the yarn in Canada — hence the name.

A substitute dubbing can be manufactured, by the tyer, by blending medium-brown, medium-green, bronze and red mohair. The substitute is then wound on the hook shank and picked out to create this very "buggy" leech pattern.

The original Canadian brown mohair yarn has become something of a legend in the Northwest and the tyers who possess skeins treat them with as much respect as a collector of fine art would a Picasso.

Using either the commercial yarn, or dubbed yarn, the tyer picks it out creating a shaggy leech.

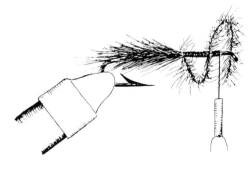

Mohair-Marabou Leech

Species: Leech.

Data
Type: Suggestive.
Line: Hi-density.
Retrieve: Hand-twist or standard.
Time: All season.

Description
Hook: Sizes 6-12, 4X long. Weighted or unweighted.
Thread: Black or Red.
Tail: Dark brown marabou.
Body: Dark brown mohair. Long strand type.
Head: Black or red.

The Henry's Lake and Canadian Brown leeches are successful and the combination of the two types is another deadly pattern. If there is anything with more action than a combination of marabou and mohair, this writer has yet to see it.

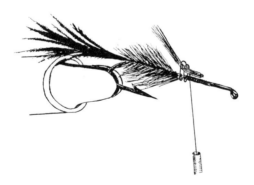

The body of these mohair patterns can be tied with two different methods. First, the mohair yarn is wrapped around the hook shank in the normal "wrap and pick out" method or, secondly, the mohair yarn is shredded and strategically placed on the shank so that it forms a flattened profile.

Chapter 30

Backswimmers

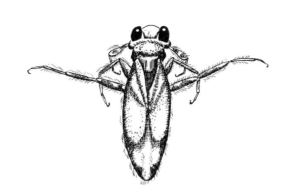

Backswimmers, canoe-bugs, water bugs — whatever one chooses to call the little stillwater Hemiptera — are among the least understood of our underwater life forms. They are active year around in most of our lakes, but are important to the angler primarily during late winter and early spring. During these times, many of our "summer nymphs" are less active, and the fly rodder should dress and fish these little bugs.

Backswimmers swim with great agility, darting here and there but always returning to the surface for oxygen. Their behavior is a rhythmic activity of hunting prey and resting to breathe, thus the angler should fish his imitations with a herky-jerky motion.

Backswimmers feed on almost any organism they can defeat. Some even prey on baitfish, snails and tadpoles.

Imitations of this species are among the best of the early season bluegill patterns. They should be fished much more slowly for bream than for trout.

Grouse Winged Backswimmer

Species: Backswimmer (Hemiptera)

Data
Type: Imitative.
Line: Floating and slow sinking.
Retrieve: Short jerky retrieve working the fly
                to the surface then letting it settle
                toward the bottom.
Time: Best during spring and early summer.

Description
Hook: Sizes 10-18, 1X long. Weighted or unweighted.
Thread: Black or brown.
Body: Dark hare's mask dubbing.
Wing case: Brown mottled feather tied in at hook
                bend and pulled shellback style
                over the body.
Legs: Two pheasant-tail fibers extended like oars
                and tied midway in body.
Head: Black or brown.

This little half-inch backswimmer probably is the most widely distributed American species. Almost every lake and pond I've fished in the West contains specimens. Other variations the tyer should include in his fly boxes are: the Corixa Bug, tied almost exactly the same but with a mottled turkey wing section as shell-back; Gray-winged Backswimmer, using a dark, slate-colored duck quill section as shellback.

Tellico

Species:	Backswimmer.

Data

Type:	Suggestive.
Line:	Floating and slow sinking.
Retrieve:	Hand twist and varied. The fly should be fished with an erratic motion to the surface, then let it settle toward the bottom.
Time:	Best during spring and early summer.

Description

Hook:	Sizes 10-14, regular shank.
Thread:	Black.
Tail:	Guinea hackle fibers. Pheasant-tail fibers may be substituted.
Body:	Bright yellow wool yarn. Ribbed with peacock herl or heavy black tying thread.
Shellback:	Pheasant-tail fibers tied on at the bend and over the top of body to eye of hook.
Hackle:	Brown hackle, soft, tied beard style.
Head:	Black.

I have found the Tellico, Prince Nymph, Zug Bug and Grouse-winged Back-swimmer fill my needs for Hemiptera species imitations. While most backswimmers (sometimes called water-boatman or canoe-bugs) are active during the entire season, it is during the spring that fly fishermen find the water bugs most effective.

It is necessary to understand their great swimming agility, in order to properly fish the little bug. They dive with rapid movements and bounce to the surface regularly. Their bouyancy is such that they cannot remain submerged without attaching themselves to a plant stem. The fly rodder should fish them with this rapid motion, pausing at times to imitate "rest periods."

Zug Bug

Species: Backswimmer.

Data
Type: Suggestive.
Line: All types.
Retrieve: All variations.
Time: All season. A particularly good early season fly.

Description
Hook: Sizes 10-14, 2X long.
Thread: Black
Tail: Four peacock sword fibers.
Body: Peacock herls, ribbed with gold or silver tinsel.
Wing case: Grouse fibers, ¼ to ½ body length.
Hackle: Brown hackle fibers tied beard style.
Head: Black.

The Zug Bug may be the best early season nymph the flytier can dress. Although it shouldn't be discounted during the summer and fall months, it is in the colder early spring water that the pattern really shines.

Prince Nymph

Species: Backswimmer.

Data
Type: Suggestive.
Line: All types.
Retrieve: All variations.
Time: All season. A good fly for early spring.

Description
Hook: Sizes 10-14, 2X long.
Thread: Black.
Tail: Brown primary, 2 fibers, stiff portion as V.
Body: Peacock herl, full body. Ribbed with silver oval tinsel.
Hackle: Brown hackle tied beard style.
Wings: White primary, 2 fibers, one on each side.
Head: Black.

This pattern originated in the Kings River area in northern California and is another early season producer.

Chapter 31

The Snail

My research for this chapter confirmed a suspicion I've had for years. Fishermen know very little about snails, other than the fact they show up in trout autopsies with amazing frequency. Flytiers have studiously avoided the little mollusks.

I began experimenting with a snail pattern several years ago and have developed a fly that has been super productive on specific occasions.

It would seem that the uncomplicated shape of the snail found in most lakes and reservoirs, would be simple to duplicate. In a sense it has been. The problem has been in "fishing" the fly. Since snails spend most of their time in fairly heavy weed beds it presents a problem of fishing strategy, not of fly pattern.

The fly fisherman must work the open pockets in weed beds, allowing his fly to settle all the way to the bottom. He then recovers line with a very slow hand twist retrieve.

I seldom admit fishing the snail-fly, if I can avoid doing so. The smirks such an admission sometimes provokes is something I can do without. But one very obvious fact of "fish-life" (the comparative ease with which fish can gather snails) has me convinced that when extremely hungry, big trout often seek out and feed heavily on the little mollusks.

So — even though most of the experts choose to ignore snails, I recommend the stillwater nymph fisherman give them strong consideration at the tying vise.

Snail

Species:	Snail.	
Data		
Type:	Imitative.	
Line:	Fast-sinking.	
Retrieve:	Dead drift. Allow pattern to settle to the bottom.	
Time:	All season.	
Description		
Hook:	Sizes 8-12, 1X short.	
Thread:	Dark olive.	
Body:	Medium size, dark olive-green chenille. Wrapped over itself to form snail shape.	
Hackle:	Dark-olive hackle, 1 turn.	
Head:	Dark olive.	

The snail pattern can be especially effective during early season before the weed beds are fully developed and snails are easily accessible.

Several good variations include: light and medium olive, light and dark brown, and grayish green.

The pattern doesn't produce results on every trip, but when it does work . . . it works with dispatch.

Chapter 32

Forage Fish

The value of streamer and bucktail fly patterns in the stillwater anglers fly books can hardly be over-emphasized. Boiling my selection down to five patterns presented a problem in direct proportion to their obvious value.

My list, therefore, is open to challenge. How, for instance, could I have left off the Mickey Finn or Art Flick's Black Nose Dace? I would be the first to admit there are dozens of excellent forage fish imitators and the angler should fish the patterns he feels comfortable with.

Stayner Ducktail

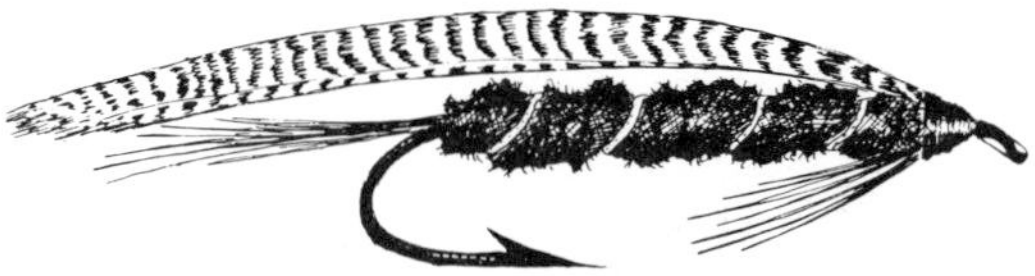

Species:	Forage fish.
Data	
Type:	Suggestive.
Line:	All types.
Retrieve:	Varied and super-quick.
Time:	All season.
Description	
Hook:	Sizes 6-14, 3X long. Weighted or unweighted.
Thread:	Black.
Tail:	Hot-orange hackle fibers.
Body:	Medium size, dark olive-green chenille, ribbed with gold oval tinsel.
Beard:	Hot-orange hackle fibers.
Wing:	Mallard flank feather, length of body and tail, tied flat.
Head:	Black.

Originated by Ruel Stayner of Twin Falls, Idaho, this pattern imitates bait fish found in many lakes and reservoirs. The Ducktail has become an integral part of my float-tube system and I recommend it highly for not only bass and trout, but also bluegill, crappie and channel catfish.

124

Large western irrigation storage reservoirs account for many really big trout.

Spruce Fly

Species:	Forage fish.

Data

Type:	Suggestive.
Line:	All types.
Retrieve:	Standard and varied.
Time:	All season.

Description

Hook:	Sizes 6-12, 2X long.
Thread:	Black.
Tail:	Peacock sword fibers.
Body:	Red floss or yarn, slender.
Shoulder:	Peacock herl.
Hackle:	Badger hackle, 3 wraps.
Wing:	Two badger hackle tips, back to back, and on edge.
Head:	Black.

This is an excellent trout fly for searching large lakes and reservoirs for rainbow, cutthroat and browns. I usually fish the fly on a deep sinking line with a varied retrieve.

125

Integration

    Species: Forage fish.

    Data
    Type: Suggestive.
    Line: All types.
    Retrieve: Standard and varied.
    Time: All season.

    Description
    Hook: Sizes 2-10, 4X long.
    Thread: Black.
    Body: Large oval silver tinsel or mylar piping.
    Wing: Black bucktail overwing; white bucktail underwing.
    Head: Black.

This fly was created by Ted Trueblood and is an excellent attractor-type streamer. The only variation from Ted's original tie I recommend is adding a splash of red hackle fibers at the throat to imitate gills.

Malheur Streamer

    Species: Forage fish.

    Data
    Type: Suggestive.
    Line: All types.
    Retrieve: Standard and varied.
    Time: All season.

    Description
    Hook: Sizes 6-10, 4X long.
    Thread: Black.
    Tail: Pheasant-tail fibers.
    Body: Orange floss, ribbed with gold oval tinsel.
    Wing: Pheasant-tail fibers, length of body and tail.
    Head: Black.

This streamer pattern was one of the first flies I received from a reader when I initiated my "Fly of the Week" feature in *The Idaho Statesman* newspaper. Named for Malheur Reservoir in Eastern Oregon, where according to the reader it was a "killer," the pattern has been successful in lakes with populations of both trout and spiney rays.

White Marabou Muddler

Species: Forage fish, particularly sculpins.

Data
Type: Suggestive.
Line: All types.
Retrieve: Standard and varied.
Time: All season.

Description
Hook: Sizes 2-10, 3X long. Weighted or unweighted.
Thread: Black or white. White for weighted patterns.
Tail: Red hackle fibers, tied medium-short.
Body: Silver-tinsel chenille.
Wing: Tie in a small bunch of gray squirrel tail
                hair and over that tie in white marabou.
Topping: Six or eight strands of peacock herl.
Hackle: Spin on collar of tannish gray deer body hair.
Head: Spin on dyed brown deer body hair and clip to
                shape. White deer body hair may be substituted.

Originated by Dan Bailey, Livingston, Montana, in 1959 to imitate a variety of minnows or forage fish. The standard variations of the marabou muddler include: black marabou over silver-tinsel chenille; brown marabou over gold tinsel-chenille; gray marabou over silver-tinsel chenille; olive marabou over gold tinsel chenille; and yellow marabou over gold-tinsel chenille.

Although some variations dye the deer hair to match the marabou used, I prefer to use natural whitetail or mule deer hair.

127

Chapter 33

Nondescripts

My Webster defines "nondescript" as: "A thing that cannot be easily described or classed." Fly patterns that fall under the nondescript classification may be a mystery to fishermen . . . but not to fish.

There long has been debate on whether fish see an object as we see it. What may look good to the fisherman may not appeal to fish. In learning to dress flies I quickly discovered the adage, "we tie two types of flies — one for the fisherman, another for the fish," is applicable to the flies the float-tuber ties.

The nondescripts described in this chapter have been tied for fish and proven, by this writer and hundreds of other float-tubers, over a decade in the field.

Stick Fly

Species:	Nondescript.
Data	
Type:	Nondescript.
Line:	Fast sinking. Often effective on a floating line with a long leader.
Retrieve:	Standard or varied with sinking line. Leisenring Lift with floating line.
Time:	All season.
Description	
Hook:	Sizes 8-12, 3X long.
Thread:	Black or brown.
Body:	Frosty brown wool, shredded and dubbed. Ribbed with silver or oval tinsel.
Head:	Black or brown.

The stick fly is a standard for float-tube fly fishermen looking for trout. The variations are infinite. I have copies of everything from variegated silver-white to speckled violet. The pattern listed above is the brain-child of another Nampa, Idaho float-tuber, Mick Miller. I've watched this fly outperform other patterns on lowland trout reservoirs too many times to discount it's value.

The only variation to Mick's original pattern, is a sparse brown hackle.

Tip: Where can you find the frosty wools and mohairs mentioned in some of my stillwater nymphs? Visit every yarn shop you can find. In my travels, I've found skeins of scarce long-haired mohair in yarn shops throughout a half dozen of the Pacific Northwest and Rocky Mountain states. I imagine yarn shops all over the country have hidden treasures for float-tube flytiers.

Tex's Favorite

Species:	Nondescript.

Data
Type:	Nondescript.
Line:	All types.
Retrieve:	Various.
Time:	All season.

Description
Hook:	Sizes 6-14, 3X long.
Thread:	Black.
Tail:	Brown hackle fibers.
Body:	Medium size, dark olive-green chenille.
Hackle:	Brown hackle, 3 wraps tied wet style.
Head:	Black.

Named for its originator, Wayne (Tex) Meeks, of Nampa, Idaho, it would be difficult to imagine a less complicated pattern. The "Tex" is legendary in Southern Idaho and should be included in every float-tuber's fly collection.

Although I don't recommend tampering with the pattern — I've tried every variation and find the original the most effective — I do carry several color combinations in my fly boxes. They include: dark-olive grizzly hackle and gray, brown, tan, light-olive, insect green, kelly-green and black chenille for the bodies.

Full Thorax Tex

Species:	Nondescript.

Data
Type:	Nondescript.
Line:	Hi-density.
Retrieve:	Various.
Time:	All season.

Description
Hook:	Sizes 8-12, 3X long.
Thread:	Black.
Tail:	Brown hackle fibers.
Body:	Small dark olive-green chenille.
Thorax:	Large size, dark olive-green chenille, twice body size.
Hackle:	Brown hackle fibers.
Head:	Black.

As with most flytiers I felt compelled to "improve" on the "Tex," so I came up with a thorax version. I won't say it catches fish any better than the original, but it does add another dimension to my group of "chenille patterns." As with the Tex, the variations are almost infinite.

A word to the beginner: "Inventing" flies is a great pastime, but improving existing patterns is a better one. I have fly boxes jammed full of originals, most of which haven't been fished. When I'm on a serious fishing trip — I guess you might say most of my trips come under that heading — I nearly always end up fishing proven patterns. Although "smelling the roses" may be great . . . catching fish is "greater."

Sheep Creek Special

Species:	Nondescript.

Data

Type:	Nondescript.
Line:	Hi-density.
Retrieve:	Various.
Time:	All season.

Description

Hook:	Sizes 6-12, 4X long. Weighted and unweighted.
Thread:	Black or brown.
Tail:	Brown hackle, 3 wraps, flared.
Body:	Medium size dark olive-green chenille.
Wing:	15 or 20 mallard flank fiber, tied to reach just short of the hackled tail.
Head:	Black or brown.

I became acquainted with this pattern during the spring of 1970. I was fishing Sheep Creek Reservoir, on the Idaho-Nevada border and not having much luck when a stranger offered to show me how to catch fish with what he called the "best fly in the book." The angler's name was George Biggs from Jerome, Idaho. He not only put on a great demonstration with the fly rod, he gave me samples of his fly.

Later when I initiated my "Fly of the Week" newspaper feature, the first pattern I ran was the Sheep Creek Special. Later when I described the fly to some friends, who also knew George, they caustically informed me it was the "Biggs Fly." Call it what you will . . . it catches fish.

Tip: Pattern dimensions should be strictly adhered to. Even slight variations can reduce the effectiveness of a fly. In the case of the Sheep Creek Special, the wing should end just short of the flared tail.

Peacock Nymph

Species:	Nondescript.

Data

Type:	Nondescript.
Line:	Various.
Retrieve:	Various.
Time:	All season.

Hook: Sizes 6-10, 4X long.
Thread: Black.
Rear hackle: Brown hackle, 3 turns, flared, should not
      reach much past point of hook.
Body: Peacock herls, medium thick.
Front hackle: Brown hackle, 3 turns, wet fly style,
      should match rear hackle.
Head: Black.

I first fished this pattern during the summer of 1972. It was given me by Colonel Bill Moberly of Cheyenne, Wyoming. Bill had at one time tied flies commercially, and considered this was his most successful pattern. I've noticed the fore-and-afts are extremely popular in the Colorado and New Mexico areas.

Chenille Fore-and-Aft

Species: Nondescript.

Data
Type: Nondescript.
Line: Various.
Retrieve.   Various.
Time: All season.

Description
Hook: Sizes 6-12, 1X long.
Thread: Black.
Rear hackle: Ginger hackle, 3 turns, flared, should reach
      just past hook point.
Body: Medium size, light-olive chenille.
Front hackle: Black hackle, 3 turns, flared, should match
      length of rear hackle.
Head: Black.

Another nondescript pattern that produces well despite the fact that it neither matches nor suggests any particular nymph. As with the more popular woolly worm and "chenille patterns," it offers the tyer an assortment of combinations limited only by one's imagination.

Carey Special

Species: Nondescript.

Data
Type: Nondescript.
Line: Fast-sinking.
Retrieve: Standard and varied.
Time: All season.

Description

Hook:	Sizes 4-12, 2X long
Thread:	Black.
Tail:	Ground hog hairs. (optional)
Body:	Ground hog hairs. Ribbed with black tying thread, reverse wound.
Hackle:	Pheasant-rump feathers, 3 wraps.
Head:	Black.

Originated by Dr. Lloyd A. Day, Quesnel, B.C., and Colonel Carey about 1925. The original name was "Monkey-Faced Louise." It was renamed the Carey Special and popularized by the late Joe Spurrier, Kelowna sporting goods dealer. It was designed to represent the caddis larva rising to hatch. Dr. Day had the idea, and Carey tied the original.

This dressing is the original, but popular variations include bodies of peacock herl, green wool or dark olive-green chenille.

Shellback Woolly Worm

Species:	Nondescript.

Data

Type:	Nondescript.
Line:	Various.
Retrieve:	Various.
Time:	All season.

Description

Hook:	Sizes 6-12, 3X long.
Thread:	Black.
Tail.	Pheasant-tail fibers.
Body:	Medium size brown chenille.
Hackle:	Brown hackle feather palmered, trimmed to ¼-inch on belly.
Shellback:	Pheasant-tail fibers.
Head:	Black.

When I ran this pattern as a "Fly of the Week," in my newspaper column I called it an "improved" woolly worm. When I later was asked how I could improve on the "best" wet fly of all, I decided to rename it.

Two important variations substitute light and dark olive-green chenille.

Carrot Nymph

Species:	Nondescript.

Data

Type:	Nondescript.
Line:	Medium sinking.
Retrieve:	Standard and varied.
Time:	All season.

Description

Hook:	Sizes 8-12, regular shank.
Thread:	Black.
Tip:	Gold Tinsel.
Body:	Orange wool, tapered larger toward head.
Hackle:	Gray and brown partridge breast feather, tied wet style.
Head:	Black.

An excellent cutthroat, rainbow and brook trout fly in small lakes.

Coon-Bug

Species:	Nondescript.

Data

Type:	Nondescript.
Line:	Fast-sinking.
Retrieve:	Various.
Time:	All season.

Description

Hook:	Sizes 2-10, 3X long.
Thread:	Tan or red.
Body:	Raccoon fur, including guard hairs, dubbed on red tying thread and wound loosely on hook shank.
Head:	Tan or red.

I first saw the Coon-Bug at Henry's Lake in the early 1970s. My guess is that fish take it for a leech.

The fly was made popular at Henry's by the late Glen Bennett, a master fly fisherman from Kansas. Glen, who passed away in the spring of 1975, was a regular for many years at Staley Springs. Those who have fished Henry's lake during the decade of the 1960s might remember Glen as the gent in the striped bib overalls with "Field and Stream" buttons all over his hat.

Woolly Worm

Species:	Nondescript.

Data

Type:	Nondescript.
Line:	All types.
Retrieve:	Various.
Time:	All year.

Description

Hook:	Sizes 4-14, 3X long. Weighted or unweighted.
Thread:	Black or brown.
Tail:	Optional, various materials.
Body:	Appropriate color of medium or large chenille. Palmered with partially clipped hackle of an appropriate color. May or may not be ribbed.
Head:	Black or brown.

The only difference between my float-tube woolly worm and the standard tie, is that I clip my hackle in a manner so as to suggest a very sparsely dressed woolly worm.

The best combinations include: dark olive-green with brown or grizzly hackle; brown with brown or black hackle; and black with black or grizzly hackle.

Bobcat

Species:	Nondescript.

Data

Type:	Nondescript.
Line:	Various.
Retrieve:	Standard or varied.
Time:	All season.

Description

Hook:	Sizes 8-12, 2X long.
Thread:	Black.
Body:	Dubbed bobcat fur, tapered slightly larger toward head.
Hackle:	Brown hackle, 2 turns.
Head:	Black.

When tying flies such as the bobcat it is a good idea to "bracket" your patterns with slightly lighter and slight darker variations. I usually add some raccoon for my lighter phase and beaver for the darker.

Mo-Nymph

Species:	Nondescript.

Data

Type:	Nondescript.
Line:	Fast-sinking.
Retrieve:	All types.
Time:	All season.

Description
Hook: Sizes 4-10, 4X long. Weighted or unweighted.
Thread: Black or brown.
Tail: Pheasant-tail fibers, natural or dyed dark olive.
                Similar materials may be substituted.
Body: Appropriate mohair yarn, shredded and dubbed
                fuller toward head. Hair is picked out at
                sides and trimmed flat on top and bottom.
Shellback: Pheasant-tail fibers, natural or dyed dark olive.
                Although the shellback is optional, I use
                it on most of my mo-nymphs.
Wing case: Pheasant-tail fibers, natural or dyed dark olive.
Head: Black or brown.

This pattern, as well as the "God-awful" are examples of the tying technique of northwestern float-tubers and demonstrates the importance of mohair yarn in their nymphs.

The best mohair colors include: Various shades of olive-green, brown, gray and tan.

The desired shape of the mo-nymph emphasizes a "flattened" body.

God-Awful

Species: Nondescript.

Data
Type: Nondescript.
Line: Fast-sinking.
Retrieve: All types.
Time: All season.

Description
Hook: Sizes 4-10, 4X long. Weighted or unweighted.
Thread: Black or brown.
Body: Dark brown and medium olive-green mohair,
                shredded and alternately dubbed fuller toward
                head. Hair is picked out on sides and trimmed
                flat on top and bottom.
Head: Black or brown.

The original was dressed by Ken Magee, Boise fly shop operator and fished successfully in many Northwestern lakes and ponds. It is interesting to note that although this pattern is considered somewhat unusual among those who dress and fish it in southern Idaho, an almost exact duplicate evolved in the Spokane, Washington area called the "Ragamuffin."

Chapter 34

Largemouth Bass and Bluegill

In dressing flies for bass and bluegill the flytier need not get complicated with his patterns. The secret in most of his spiney ray patterns should be simplicity. His largemouth flies should be as big as the tyer can dress them. He should make good use of marabou and other easy to cast materials, and his creations should imitate minnows, eels and frogs.

His bluegill flies should also be simple. The key to nymph fishing for bream is in the presentation — more than in the pattern.

Serpentine

Species: Nondescript.

Data
Type: Nondescript.
Line: Floating or slow sinking.
Retrieve: Various.
Time: All season.

Description
Hook: Sizes 1/0-6, 3X long.
Thread: Black.
Tail: Four extra long black saddle hackles.
Body: Black saddle hackles palmered tightly together on the bare hook shank.
Collar: Two hot-orange saddle hackles the same size as body.
Head: Black.

To catch lunker largemouth, the fly fisherman must offer the fish something "worthwhile." The largemouth seems to have a built in computer that tells him when the calories in a morsel are worth expending energy. The serpentine is one of the few dressings that gives the lake and pond float-tuber a weapon with which he can expect to catch hawg-bass.

The only variation I use calls for purple neck hackles in place of black.

Marabou Mess

Species: Nondescript.

Data
Type: Nondescript.
Line: Floating or sinking.
Retrieve: Various.
Time: All season.

Description
Hook: Sizes 1/0-4, keel hook, weighted.
Thread: Black.
Tail: Black marabou, large clump.
Body: Gold-tinsel chenille.
Wing: Black marabou, large clump.
Head: Bead eyes, black thread.

An excellent fly to "deep probe" for largemouth or smallmouth. A little bulky to cast but effective on large fish.

A somewhat "lighter" version consists of a marabou tail and wing with a chenille body.

Bass Fluff-Butt

Species: Nondescript.

Data
Type: Nondescript.
Line: Sinking.
Retrieve: Various.
Time: All season.

Description
Hook: Sizes 2-6, 6X long. Weighted or unweighted.
Thread: Black.
Tail: A large clump of black (or appropriate color) marabou.
Body: Large black chenille (or appropriate color.) May be palmered with black saddle hackle. Two wraps of hot-orange chenille may be added at head.
Head: Black.

Another "large" bass fly. With marabou of the proper length on a number 2, 6X hook, we can show largemouth a morsal almost 5-inches long.

Mohair Crayfish

Species: Crayfish.

Data
Type: Suggestive.
Line: Hi-density.
Retrieve: Various.
Time: All season.

Description
Hook: Sizes 2-8, 4X long. Weighted.
Thread: Brown.
Tail: Rust-brown mohair, tapered.
Body: Rust-brown mohair, larger toward pincers.
Legs: Pheasant-tail fibers, tied at each side.
Pincers: Pheasant-tail fibers, tied in a "V" at the bend of the hook.
Head: Pheasant-tail fibers, trimmed short at bend of hook. The tyer must remember the crayfish swims backwards, so the pattern must be tied backwards.

Although the mohair may be applied by simply wrapping the yarn, I prefer to shred the yarn and form a new "yarn" with the loop tying method, or by placing clumps of mohair on each side of the shank, as described on page 118.

Skunk Fluff-Butt

Species: Nondescript.

Data
Type: Nondescript.
Line: Various.
Retrieve: Hand twist.
Time: All season.

Description
Hook: Sizes 8-14, 3X long.
Thread: Black.
Tail: White marabou, body length.
Body: Black chenille.
Shellback: White marabou.
Head: Black.

The key to nymph fishing for bluegill can be summed up in two words . . . "fish slowly!" Bluegill seldom follow a fly far unless they are on their spawning beds. I have a novel retrieve that works when bream are extra lazy. I let my fly sink as deeply as I think necessary and turn my tube very slowly, allowing the rod tip to move the fly at a slow, steady speed. When I've completed a 45 degree turn, without a strike, I strip in line, turn toward my fly and repeat the maneuver.

Bee

Species: Nondescript.

Data
Type: Nondescript.
Line: Various.
Retrieve: Hand twist.
Time: All season.

Description
Hook: Sizes 8-12, regular shank.
Thread: Black.
Body: Rear half black chenille, front half yellow chenille.
Hackle: Black hackle feather, two turns.

I once read an article that said color wasn't important in a bluegill pattern . . . as long as it was yellow and black. After fishing the bee for several seasons, I'm not sure but what that wasn't an accurate evaluation.

Sponge Spider

Species: Nondescript.

Data
Type: Nondescript.
Line: Various.
Retrieve: Hand twist.
Time: All season.

Description
Hook: Sizes 8-12, regular shank.
Thread: Black.
Body: Green sponge, cut and shaped.
Legs: White rubber strips.
Head: Black.

While there are several color variations the bream fisherman can dress for his sport, the best include: black body with white legs; white body with black or white legs; black and yellow and yellow and black.

While I list only three specific bluegill patterns there are others I consider indispensible. These include: all the mayfly nymphs and caddis pupas; damsel nymphs; backswimmers; Stayner Ducktail; Zug Bug; Prince Nymph; and Tex's Favorite.

I dress my bluegill patterns in sizes ranging from 8 to 16.

Epilog

The Old Fisherman

It was warm for a December day.

The sun's rays slipped in and out of the puffy white clouds overhead. On the horizon, puffy white clouds were turning grayish-blue. The winds created "overhangs" on the ridges that held the sand in vertical cliffs along the tops of the dunes, causing the southern sun to cast shadows that dramatically changed their character.

The old man studied the scene for several minutes. He couldn't remember the middle dune being so high or so steep. It had been many years since he had last climbed the big dunes, and the impluse to do so this fine December afternoon was repressed quickly.

The old fisherman trudged around West Dune and across the marsh until he reached his favorite lagoon. A gaggle of Canadian geese that had been floating languidly just beyond a reed island broke and flew when they realized their solitude was no longer inviolate. A hen mallard quacked the alarm and quickly joined the geese in flight.

The old man briefly admired the birds in flight, then dropped his gear to the ground and stooped to pick up a handful of water. "Too cold," he muttered to himself, "too cold to catch fish."

The old fisherman watched the water for a time and couldn't see any fish activity although now and then he could see minute midges popping to the surface. The old man knew the fish probably would feed some time during the day — he only hoped they hadn't already satisfied their meager December appetites.

He assembled his favorite bluegill rod, attached a small, white, rubber-legged spider and set to fishing.

After a dozen or so fruitless casts, he stopped fishing and propped his Payne rod up against a nearby Russian olive and himself against another. The suns rays were beginning to make him drowsy — a symbol more of the time of the year than of the age of the fisherman.

A nearby gray squirrel hesitated for a moment, then realizing the old man was indeed it's benefactor, sidled up and nervously began searching the old man's coat pockets. It was a game the two had played many times before. A game in which the squirrel always came away the winner.

A breeze riffled the Russian olives, and the old man's fly rod, caught by an especially strong gust, thudded to the ground. The old fisherman remained still . . . unhearing.

The squirrel skipped off with both cheeks full of nuts, searching for a safe place to bury them. The afternoon sun would drop much closer to the horizon before the squirrel would return.

The lakes usually were deserted this time of the year. Now and then, a die-hard angler would leave prints in the sand . . . but not often.

The shadow of the high dune reached the shoreline across the lake and almost obscured the presence of a pair of coyotes making their way along the lake in search of an evening meal. In the distance, the sound of another coyote caused the pair to hesitate. Then completely unaware of the presence of the old fisherman, the pair continued their hunt.

Over the marsh, a pair of chicken hawks fluttered in hunting formation, now and then darting down as if teasing their prey. When one hawk scored a kill, the other became more intense in its activity.

The sun reached lower on the horizon, almost touching the rim of the canyon. The sound of a flock of honkers announced their return to the lake, certain in their limited intelligence that the intruder was gone.

The old fisherman did not move.

A trio of pintails wheeled into the lagoon in search of temporary quarters before the evening feeding hour.

The gray squirrel returned to the old fisherman, again searching his pockets. The pockets yielded no nuts. Bouncing away, the furry animal climbed into the lower branches of one of the nearby olive trees.

Over the rim of the canyon, the puffy white clouds had completely mingled with the blue-grays. A chill came over the dunes. The squirrel blinked, cocking it's head from side to side, aware that something important had happened but not quite sure what.

At the far end of the lake, a loon signaled its arrival. Overhead flights of mallards heading for corn fields grew larger.

The gray squirrel dropped from its perch and once again searched the old man's pockets. It found a final nut. Squinting one last time at the still figure of the old fisherman, the squirrel tucked the nut into it's cheek and scampered off.

A long fishing season had come to an end.

Index